Snap to Whistle

VIEWING ADVERSITY AS AN OPPORTUNITY TO GROW

KEVIN DONLEY

ISBN: 978-1-4834-8923-0 (sc)
ISBN: 978-1-4834-8922-3 (e)

Library of Congress Control Number: 2018908862

Lulu Publishing Services rev. date: 08/14/2018

Acknowledgements

In the accomplishment of any task there are always many, many others without whose help, contribution, support, and/ or efforts would never happen. The achievements in this book could never have been done without them. I want to especially thank my wife Rita for her patience and support in this endeavor. Her suggestions and editorial help were invaluable. I want to thank my son Patrick, my daughter Megan, and all my family for their patience, encouragement, and assistance throughout. They have been a constant source of strength and sustenance.

The success of this program was built on the generous friendship and backing of several families and individuals. I personally want to thank the Jehl Family, the Shields Family, the McKibben Family, and the Busse Family for their help and encouragement in the building of the Saint Francis program from its inception. Without their generous and unwavering help none of this would have been possible. I want to thank and give recognition to University of Saint Francis President Sister Elise Kriss for her unbending support and sharing of a dream of what football could mean and become for the university.

No group of individuals sacrificed and contributed more to our success than the USF football coaches who devoted so much of their time and efforts to help make Cougar football a success and cause for community pride. No football program or team would ever be successful without their dedication, sacrifices, and hard work. The same applies to the many, many young men who have chosen to come to Saint Francis, put on a Cougar uniform, and spend endless hours and all their energy and efforts to create the success we've come to expect. Finally, I want to thank Jerry Lawson for his efforts in helping me write this book and get it into print.

Table of Contents

PART III POST-GAME LESSONS

Introduction

The purpose of this book is to share some real life experiences with you, the reader, of the initial twenty years of a college football program that may be applicable to your life journey.

It's been a twenty-year sentimental journey of the ups and downs and growth and maturity of eighteen to twenty-two year-olds that has become a 100 x 53½ yard piece of heaven, and I want to express a special tribute to the many young men who have earned the silver helmet honor and committed four years of their lives in striving for excellence and representing our great University.

I would also like to recognize and give thanks to the coaches, faculty, sisters, and administrators who have been part of the monitoring and educating our wonderful young men. I also want thank and recognize the players and coaches' families for the sacrifice and support they have unselfishly given over the past two decades. I also want to thank and recognize the countless friends of the community who have been such an integral part of the program and University growth. Lastly, I want to give thanks to God for ongoing direction and always having our back.

The twenty-year growth of this football program has matured from victories and championships to personal development of the individuals as it relates to character development and purpose with discovery of commitment and unselfish maximum effort, which is the foundation of any successful team, university, or business.

I hope you enjoy the story of our jubilant journey and you are able to find the parallels for your own life.

KD

PART ONE

TWO MINUTES TO GAME TIME

Chapter 1

Taking Flight

In football, the "snap to whistle" is those few seconds between the hiking of the football and the referee blowing his whistle to signal the end of the play. It is within that brief span of time all the action takes place. A hundred decisions are made, some good, some bad, and each one affecting the outcome.

A single snap-to-whistle moment in my life, when I was fifty-three changed everything. It was two minutes in a lifetime of minutes, in which one decision completely recalibrated the path I was taking.

On a hot July morning in 2004 I boarded a puddle jumper to fly from Fort Walton Beach, Florida, to Atlanta and then grab a connecting flight to Indiana. I had been visiting my aged parents, both in their eighties, and was eager to get back

1

to Fort Wayne and to the University of Saint Francis so I could focus on football and the new season ahead.

Working at St. Francis had been a humbling experience. I had once been on top of the world as one of the most successful coaches in college football before being hired by a school that didn't even have a football team and was counting on me to put more than cobwebs in the trophy case.

St. Francis was a chance at redemption for me. Before that job, I had been fired, homeless, and aimless. That was past I had finally started to feel good about myself and the progress the team had made in six years. It was what mattered.

Until that flight.

Because Elgin Air Force Base is near Fort Walton Beach, several military personnel were on the forty-five-minute flight. I boarded, settled into my seat and once the plane was in the air, started making small talk with the air force officer occupying the seat next to me. Fifty minutes passed. Sixty. Eighty. I glanced over at my seatmate. "Shouldn't we be landing here pretty soon?"

I expected the officer to give me some answer about Atlanta being a busy place or how aircraft sometimes had to circle and get in line to wait for permission to land. Instead, the officer's brow creased, and his voice lowered. "We're in trouble."

You know that feeling in the pit of your stomach when you're about to ask a question you don't really want answered? That was how I felt in the next few seconds. "What do you mean, we're in trouble?"

"We're dropping fuel." The officer pointed out the window at a long white stream trailing behind the wing.

My stomach dropped. The normally forty-five-minute flight had taken twice as long and the expression on the officer's face told me he was right—we were in trouble. The plane began to fill with murmurs, nervous chatter. The fasten seatbelts sign dinged on, and then the pilot's steady, stern voice came over the speakers. "All military personnel are asked to proceed to the rear of the aircraft."

A dozen men got up and moved to the back of the plane where they began receiving instructions while everyone else was moved forward. I could feel panic rising in my gut. I had been scared before—once I chaperoned college coeds on a summer research trip to Costa Rica and had to protect them when we were besieged by drug smugglers wanting to kidnap the girls—but this fear was bone-deep, almost paralyzing.

"We are experiencing hydraulic difficulties," the pilot said. His voice never shook, never wavered. "The landing gear will not descend and the flaps on the wings won't come down so we are unable to slow the aircraft. Prepare yourselves for an emergency landing."

The flight attendants stayed calm, reciting those emergency instructions you never pay attention to until you need them. All around me, people began to cry. All I kept thinking was: *We're going down. We're going to crash.*

Out the window, I could see a thick layer of foam, like a lawn of shaving cream, being applied to the runway. When I played college ball, a three-hundred-pound linebacker once tackled me. I got scared when I hit the ground, thinking I'd broken something vital because for a moment I couldn't breathe. In that moment on the plane, while I watched the shaving cream stack up and realized it wasn't there to cushion our landing but rather to tame the fireball the plane would become, I couldn't breathe. I couldn't act. I could only think.

I thought of my job, of the players waiting for me back home. Of my family, my son and daughter. Of the mistakes I had made, the choices that had hurt others. Of how far I had strayed from the God I had once loved. And even though I wasn't sure He was going to listen to me, I whispered to God, praying to survive, to have a chance to change my life, to become the man God wanted me to be.

As the plane bucked in the rough air and the airline personnel yelled, "Heads down! Stay down!" I reached in my pocket and took out a piece of paper. I scribbled a few lines to my kids and my family, telling them I loved them. And then because I didn't want my kids to worry about what happened to me in the afterlife, I added, "I'm okay with God. Dad." Except I wasn't so sure in that moment I was okay with God. I folded the paper and carefully placed it back in my wallet, and then back in my pocket, hoping it wouldn't be burned up in the crash.

Then I closed my eyes and whispered another prayer. I told God that I accepted whatever He had waiting in the moments ahead. I accepted my fate because it was outside my control. I couldn't steer the plane safely. I couldn't control the impact. I couldn't do anything other than trust God's hands would be there to catch us.

I braced myself in my seat; head between my arms, ironically tucked into myself like a football under a quarterback's arm. The plane did a Pete Rose belly slide, screeching along the concrete runway, shuddering and bouncing forward for what seemed like forever. Foam sprayed against the windows, blurred the sight of the ground.

In that moment when the plane finally stilled and the exit slide deployed, I found the God I had been seeking all my life. For decades, I had been scrambling to maintain control—over my career, my family, myself—only to find out in the space of two minutes that control is an illusion. In that snap-to-whistle moment on the plane between the moment I braced myself and when the plane slid to a stop, I handed control of the ball to God and let Him make whatever play He wanted.

And that, I have said a thousand times in speeches to my players, is what saved my life—and more importantly, what saved me from myself.

Chapter 2

Youngest Head Coach

The traditional way to win a game is with a good running play plan. The offense keeps inching the ball further down the field, while the defensive team gets worn out chasing it, and the clock winds down. The running play is traditional because it works. It's dependable, it's simple, and it keeps your defensive line fresh for coming in after a turnover.

My life was pretty much a running play—traditional, unremarkable, and normal. I was born and raised in Springfield, Ohio, a midsized blue-collar city in the American Midwest, south of Columbus and squeezed between Dayton and Cincinnati. I grew up in a noisy, busy Irish Catholic neighborhood, where scrappy fights sprung up every day. I learned to be tough, to stand up for myself.

I was a bit of a wild child, and my parents sent me to a Catholic school to learn discipline—in those days, usually at the business end of a paddle. My dad was a decorated World War II veteran, and when he passed, my mother eventually remarried, to a retired air force colonel. I had family all around me—grandparents, aunts, uncles, and cousins. I went to church and served as an altar boy, but I wasn't a religious kid. God was this being somewhere in the ether watching over me, but that was all.

In Springfield, the world revolved around football. The whole town closed down on Friday nights, the football stadium filled up, and ten thousand people crowded onto the bleachers. Football was a world unto itself.

For three years in high school, I played linebacker. I started as quarterback and moved to running back, did the kicking, and never came off the field. I was young and enthusiastic, and when I broke my ankle in my junior year, I cut the cast off, taped the ankle and returned to the field. I broke my nose once and went right back out to play.

Even though I was recruited by the University of Dayton I didn't go there because a friend a year or so older was killed in

Vietnam, and I was devastated. I was determined to sign up to go to Vietnam, but my parents talked me out of it—and what I really wanted to do more than play was coach. I'd watch games and analyze the plays, the coach's decisions, the way those choices turned a game around. I was amazed by what coaches like Ara Parseghian and Bo Schembechler could do for a team.

The teams I loved were disciplined, but so were their opponents. They all practiced, ran plays, watched films. The more I watched, the more I realized winning wasn't necessarily about the discipline and practice it was about an indefinable, unquantifiable mystique. I was a Notre Dame fan and I always thought there was something special about that place. They knew how to win. They seemed to possess that little bit of…magic. I guess you'd call it that put one team in the winner's circle. Like in the 1970 Cotton Bowl between Texas led by Darrow Royal and Notre Dame, when underdog Notre Dame pulled something magic together and beat the unbeatable Texas Longhorns. My cousin was captain of that team. An epic game that people are still talking about more than forty years later.

That same kind of indefinable magic brought me to Anderson College. A high school coach I knew took me there on a weekend got me in and signed up and on the team.

It took me a few years and a lot of social probations before I settled in at Anderson, which was a sleepy church-based school. Nobody drank there and the culture was the total opposite of the hard living, hard loving Irish Catholic home I'd left behind. But I was happy—I loved the school, loved football, and loved my life.

I graduated and coached high school football for three years, and then Anderson called and asked me to come back as a coordinator. I was making good money at the high school—$14,000 a year, which was big bucks back in the early 1970s. Anderson offered me a dorm room, a meal ticket, a Subaru, a gas card for recruiting, $500 for expenses, and a $10,000 salary. It was a college-level coaching opportunity and I couldn't turn it down.

I was assistant coach for two years and then they offered me the head-coaching job. I was twenty-six years old. So young, but the school still expected big things out of me. Anderson hadn't won a game since I was hired as assistant coach, but for some crazy reason they put me in charge. The president said he saw something in me and he believed I could turn the program around.

I didn't know if I could do it, but I said yes anyway and became the youngest head college football coach in America in 1978. That honor lasted about a year until NFL coaching great George Allen's son, George, was hired as a head coach the next year. He was only twenty-three. Youngest or not the pressure on me to pull off a miracle was huge.

It took some doing but I turned that program around. My first year as head coach Anderson had a 6-4 win-loss record and then went to 7-3 following year. Later the team went on to win the conference championship.

When I was a kid fighting for my place in the neighborhood I learned that sometimes the best thing you can do is get up when you're down and keep on fighting. That's how I approached Anderson—they were down but they needed to get up and keep fighting. Attitude, discipline, and a little magic came together at that school and taught me lessons that turned around my life—and that of dozens of young people—many years later.

However, it was a lesson I didn't learn soon enough to save me from being on the street with all of my possessions in a couple of garbage bags. But first there was Kentucky and then Pennsylvania, and a wake-up call that told me in my rush to get to the goal post I'd lost sight of what was truly important on the field.

Chapter 3

Confidence Precedes Success

At twenty-six, a man is cocky and too self-assured. He doesn't have enough life experience to know he's got a lot of learning to do before he becomes a true adult. That was me when I took the job at Anderson. I believed I knew football better than anybody and that I had the secret none of my predecessors had. Looking back, I realize all the things I didn't know. I think the good Lord took care of me by keeping me from screwing up too badly.

Part of what made me cocky was winning. I had success early, 32-8 in the four years in my first head-coaching job at Anderson. I won right away and kept right on winning. I look back now and realize it wasn't necessarily me as a coach—it was the team. The effort was there, the excitement was there, and most of all, a positive attitude. That's what created the wins and brought success to the entire football program. It took quite a few years for me to realize that just because I was winning didn't mean I knew anything. I won a couple conference titles though and that was enough to get me my next job.

After four years at Anderson I accepted a job at Georgetown College in Kentucky. They played another division up which meant the team faced a little tougher competition. I was the seventh coach in seven years at that school, and that tells you how smart I was taking on such a project. Obviously something wasn't quite right, but I thought I could win anywhere and moved south to Kentucky.

In my interview the university asked me if I could bring this losing team up to .500. I said yes. I mean I'd done it before, right?

The first year my team won two games. *Two.*

I had coached like I coached at Anderson, but the results were different. Why? It's because teams are different and I hadn't taken that variable into account. Not all teams are constructed the same. So many factors go into assembling just the right mix of players—background, education, and access to programs, school and parental support.

What I found when we began my first spring practice at Georgetown was a pretty good clue as to why Georgetown had not been successful on the football field. Forty guys showed up. What a ragtag outfit they were! They were trying to recruit athletes with no regard for character or other qualities and the result was a lot of kids who were on the questionable side of the character divide.

Finding talented athletes who have the right character and attitude isn't something you can do as easily as ordering a pizza. It takes time to recruit—time at other schools, watching games, time in the office watching films, and time interviewing the kids, looking for that magic spark.

Time I didn't have because I was busy trying to get the team I had to win a few. In my first four years, I managed to create a competitive team, with a 4-6 record, but not a winning team. After four years we still hadn't had a winning season, but I knew we were on the right track. We were getting good kids and the scores started going up.

But it wasn't fast enough. The president who hired me left after the first year due to ill health. After finishing 4-6 in my fourth year I received a summons to the President's office. I had promised to get the team to .500, and we were close. I knew we had made significant progress, changed the way things were done, changed the culture, changed attitudes, and were on the right track. The president informed me I was fired. "We're going to go in a different direction," he said. "We want to get this football program up and going,"

I was devastated. I had two young children, a family to support, a life in Kentucky, and in an instant it was gone. Maybe I had promised them more than I ended up delivering. Part of that was the cockiness of youth and part of it I was did not know what I was stepping into. Seven coaches in seven years wasn't an accident—it was a mark of how much work the entire football program needed to get it up to speed. Worst of all I knew we were at a tipping point that we were about to reap the rewards for all the hard work I and my staff had been doing to build a successful program. It was being taken away at the moment everything was coming to fruition.

But there's more to the drama and fate intervened. When I first went to Georgetown there was a wide chasm between athletic staff and faculty. The kids on the teams weren't 'A' students. Most of them weren't even 'C' students. But I started really hammering the kids about the importance of grades and slowly the athletes turned a corner. One of my athletes graduated and went on to become a Rhodes scholar.

Those changes and that emphasis on education as the foundation of everything earned the respect of the faculty. Right after I was fired two faculty members who had once been my biggest critics went to the president and demanded I be retained. They had a petition in hand and they told him they didn't care if Georgetown never won a football game, because they were now getting the type of student athlete they wanted at the university. They were getting motivated kids who saw the importance of good grades and of committing to their education, and ultimately, their futures. In the long run that was what mattered. I got fired in the morning and rehired that same afternoon. It was a miraculous turn of events.

The next season my team at Georgetown finally changed direction and started winning games. We finished the season

6-4. The following year the team won their first conference championship, and appeared in post-season play for the first time in the school's history.

We went on to win the NAIA National Title in 1991. We played on national television and I was named National Coach of the Year. My head was in the clouds.

Those wins, that award, and the prestige that felt like such a gift at the time it happened soon became an albatross that nearly cost me everything. Coaching wasn't about the coach or about titles or awards. It was about the team—about molding young people who would become great people. Not just great football players.

Chapter 4

Falling Down

In that window between signing a letter of intent and National Signing Day every top college football player in the country is dreaming big. They are in that perfect bubble where anything can happen, any team can call their name, and the future before them seems bright and endless. The hush in the room when the picks are finally made is almost palpable, because in that instant lives are changed.

At the end of 1991 I was on top of the world. My success at Georgetown had attracted attention and several schools came courting carrying big offers. I weighed many options and ended up taking a job at the University of California in California, Pennsylvania.

California, Pennsylvania is a small town south of Pittsburgh that sits alongside the Monongahela River. With a population of less than 6,700 at the time the area was economically depressed, but the school was state supported and well funded.

The school had gone fifteen years without a winning season and like Georgetown had been through four coaches in four years. They were hungry to win and had seen what I had done in Kentucky so they offered to triple my salary assuming I could bring the same level of achievement to their program.

I was still coming off the high of winning a national title and I was cocky and overly confident. My Coach of the Year award whispered that I had what it took to assemble a team that would bring home win after win on those crisp fall afternoons. I had forgotten that moment in the Georgetown president's office the hard work and effort and the losing years I had endured before finally finding success on the field.

I figured if I could pull off a winning season at Cal U I would be recruited to work at a big school. I was forty and as much as I thought I had it all figured out—I didn't. I got caught up in the excitement of getting hired and moving into a new environment and missed the harsh realities underlying the new job.

Fifteen consecutive losing seasons had created tremendous pressure to win. The problem was that turning Cal U into a winning team wasn't as easy as heading out onto the field and pulling off some great plays. For one the football team was a second cousin to the basketball team that had a full complement of scholarships and coaches. The money at Cal U was behind the basketball team not so much the football program that left me with fewer resources than I'd expected. The school essentially wanted a miracle with no support—and they wanted that miracle yesterday.

Because of that I didn't have the time to build the team from the ground up like I had before. Instead of looking for character first and talent second I had to find the biggest, fastest, and strongest athletes. All that mattered was what the score read at the end of the game.

There was no time to focus on grades and on developing the players as good young men. It was a quick fix to produce results.

It didn't work. Working backwards and looking at the players' ability before their character meant I ended up with a lot of kids on my team who were abusing drugs. The drug culture at Cal U was pervasive, involving students, players, and many others.

Players would show up so high it was like they were from another planet. When they came down from the high they were useless. I was wasting my words trying to teach these players to be responsible young people, because they'd just turn around and do more drugs. So I implemented consequences— if one of my players was caught doing drugs I kicked him off the team.

The administration, however, was only looking at the scoreboard. I'd kick a kid off the team and they'd give him a scholarship anyway.

I was frustrated by the lack of support from the top down and decided the team needed a huge wake-up call. One afternoon I locked the doors to the gym and did mandatory drug testing on the players and coaches. The administration was furious and told me I had violated the players' civil rights.

The NCAA requires a 24-hour advance notice on all drug testing. I knew that, but I also knew these kids were smart. They knew enough to work around the test and beat it if they had prior notice about being tested. The NCAA's drug testing policy is antiquated and does little to curb the drug problem in college sports.

The administration called me on the carpet. I had been at Cal U for four seasons, had won dozens of games but they didn't care. They fired me.

I was devastated. I had gone into the job with big dreams and a track record that other coaches envied. But I couldn't see the forest for all the trees or the trees for all the forest. In the wake of all those awards and wins I had lost sight of what it took to get to the top, and most of all I had lost sight of what was important.

I'd taken a shortcut but in the end I'd failed because shortcuts don't make for consistent, sustainable success. I'd gotten so bogged down in the numbers I had failed to develop relationships with the community, alumni, administration, coaching staff, and more importantly, with the players.

It was a harsh lesson and reality check. A wake-up call of my own. I had good intentions, but I had neglected to keep things in perspective and to prioritize character over performance. A team isn't built on the fastest throws or the best kicks—it's built from young people who are committed to being good people. There are no shortcuts to creating that kind of attitude.

Most of all, I had lost sight of what was important in my own life. That day I not only lost my job, but I lost everything else that mattered to me.

Chapter 5

Bouncing Back

On a snowy, cold January night in 1997 I boarded a Greyhound bus carrying two garbage bags that held everything I owned. I'll never forget the look on my children's faces when I got on the bus and watch them sobbing as the bus pulled away and my heart shattered. I sat in the stiff, cold seat, with the smell of exhaust filling the cabin of the bus, and left my life in Pennsylvania behind.

In that moment, I was a failure. I didn't own a car. I didn't have a job. I'd lost my family, and imploded my marriage. I spent the next twenty-two hours that seemed more like a month crammed into that small space, doing nothing but thinking.

How had it gone so wrong? Four years earlier I was a married father of two, National Coach of the Year, and on top of the world. Now I was unemployed, alone, and homeless on a bus bound for my brother's house in Chicago where at least I'd have a roof over my head.

My self-esteem and self-worth were at their lowest. I had failed as a coach, failed as a husband, failed as a father, and failed as a man. I was forty-four years old and so low I wasn't even on a rung on the ladder.

General George Patton once said, "I don't measure a man's success by how high he climbs but how high he bounces when he hits bottom." I was at the bottom, and I had no choice but to rise again. The question was whether I had what it took to climb out of this pit. The fall was over. It was time to bounce. Adversity is there to be overcome. Hiding somewhere was waiting opportunity.

All these years, I'd been telling my players to view adversity as an opportunity. That speech sounded a lot different to my own ears and not so easy to do. As I rode across the snowy Midwest I realized my job had never been about a dozen Saturday afternoons in the fall. It was about developing relationships with young people so I could teach them how to become the best they could be. My job as a coach wasn't about winning football games—the winning takes care of itself if the process is right. In the end what matters is leaving the world with better human beings. Somehow I had to use that lesson to turn my life around and find another job.

Thank God for my family. My brother put me up for several months, helped me get a car, and reassured me on those dark, lonely nights that it would all work out. My mother called me daily, checking on me, supporting me. If I hadn't had my family, I'm not so sure I would have ended up where I did.

During the day I'd send out resumes and make phone calls. One of the calls I made was to my best friend of thirty years, Terry Hoeppner. At the time, Terry was the assistant football coach at Miami University of Ohio. He later went on to become the head football coach at Miami and then the head football coach at Indiana University.

Terry mentioned that he'd heard a small, Catholic college in his hometown in Indiana was looking for a football coach, but the opportunity came with a problem and a challenge.

The school had no football program. I'd be building it from the ground up.

I sent out my resume anyway and almost immediately got a call for an interview. They flew me down to Fort Wayne and drove me to the campus of Saint Francis College (it wouldn't become the University of Saint Francis until the following year). Fort Wayne looked like a nice community, a decent place to live. Saint Francis however was as Terry had warned me a small Catholic college with an enrollment of maybe six hundred students. No football field. No locker rooms. Not a single football player in the mix.

On top of that, the college was struggling financially. Enrollment was down, budgets were tight, and there was a lot of internal opposition to starting a football team. They worried that football players would disturb the serenity of the sleepy campus.

Saint Francis was at the bottom, just like me. They were desperate and hoping that adding a football program would turn the school around. They didn't care so much about winning as bringing in more students. The committee I talked to didn't want to build facilities. They wanted to practice on a nearby high school field and have the players keep their equipment in their dorm rooms.

I knew there was no way that could work. I couldn't understand why God had sent me to this school with no money and no real plan. I had always wanted to start a football program from the ground up—but I'd wanted to do it with resources, support, and money. Saint Francis had very little of any of that.

What they did have was a great community, strong academic programs, and a solid reputation with a committed faculty and good people. I liked the people I met there. And when I found out the student enrollment was 90% female I realized I'd have one more plus when I was recruiting.

Still I hesitated. Yeah I was unemployed, but did I want to accept a job from a college that might not be there by my first day? Ultimately I thanked them, turned them down, and flew back to Chicago.

And that would have been it except Saint Francis didn't give up on me that easily. When I got home I got a phone call from the twenty-nine-year-old athletic director (who had been the residence hall director two months earlier). "We want you to be the football coach," he said.

I said no again and when he asked me why I was declining I told him the school didn't understand what it would take to have a football team. They only saw it as a way to attract more students.

I got another phone call the next day from the young athletic director. "We'd really like to talk with you again," he said, "because everyone here thinks you're the strongest candidate and would be by far the best person to start a football program here at Saint Francis. So why don't you show us what it would take? Outline the program and tell us how it should be done."

I took a week wrote down a plan and flew back there. No one on the committee had enough experience with football to know if the plan was a good one or a bad one so they couldn't commit. I still wasn't sure what they saw in me or why they wanted me of all the coaches in the country to head this up. I had a national title under my belt and twenty years of experience—but I'd also been fired from my last job and had been floundering around for a while looking for another.

Saint Francis, however, needed me and frankly I needed them too. I was still unemployed and getting more worried with each passing week I was still without a job. I agreed to be a consultant on a month-to-month basis as they got the program off the ground. Meanwhile I kept on sending out resumes and making calls.

By this time it was early March. Saint Francis wouldn't start playing until 1998, but they wanted to bring in twenty football players that fall to redshirt. That would give the players time to adapt to the combined training and academic schedule, and get them ready to play the following year.

The University of Saint Francis is affiliated with the Roman Catholic Church and run by the Sisters of Saint Francis of Perpetual Adoration. The first time I met the college president, Sister Elis (Kriss), she said, "Nice to meet you, but you weren't my first choice."

I blinked. "Did I misunderstand? The committee told me I was their first choice."

"Before we chose you, we tried to get Lou Holtz, but he wouldn't return our emails." She smiled at me and joked, "It's okay. You're better looking than him anyway."

I liked Sister Elis on the spot. It didn't take long for me to figure out that she was a woman of God, committed to her faith, but also deeply committed to Saint Francis. She had a vision for the school and for what she hoped it would become.

We talked for hours that day. I shared my plan for starting a college football program, and how I saw that helping Saint Francis to grow.

She gave me her blessing and full support. We both knew that it was going to be an uphill battle. At the time all we had was a few hundred students, a vision, and a dream, but not much money. My first recruiting advance check from the college bounced and for a second I wondered what I had gotten myself into.

I wasn't much better off than the school. I went from living in my brother's basement to living in an empty college dorm, and then to a small empty storage building that was really just a condemned shack. The only way forward for both the college and me was to find some money somewhere and increase enrollment. That spring we only had about seventy kids living on campus and only about a hundred and fifty student athletes.

I wasn't having much luck recruiting either. It was mid-spring and at that time of year you're lucky if you find a couple kids who may have played a little touch football in the backyard and want to take a risk on being part of the start of something.

I was at my rock bottom and so were they but together I knew we were going to create something incredible. Sister Elis had a vision and a dream for the school and my dream complemented hers so the team started. She and I were the first two members.

Chapter 6

Building the Program Brick by Brick

The Wildcat Formation (so named for the Kansas State Wildcats, whose coaches developed the play) is one of those offensive moves designed to confuse the defensive team. Instead of snapping to the quarterback the center delivers the ball to another player (a running back or fullback). The wildcat formation is a step a little outside the conventional playbook and can create an opportunity for the offense to gain some yardage in the confusion.

Starting a football team from the ground up is a little like a wildcat play. There is no one right way to do it there are turns that take you by surprise, and you have to be ready to adapt quickly to make the most of what's in front of you. When I walked into Saint Francis I figured I had turned losing teams around more than once—how hard could it be to do the same, but with the advantage of building the entire program up from the bottom?

I went into Saint Francis with optimism, which was quickly chased by reality when I arrived. My first office was in the old Padua Hall (located in the same place of the current hall of the same name). It was a dorm built around World War II and by the time I arrived in 1997 had been condemned and was awaiting demolition.

I had to stand up to use the phone on the wall. There were bats, mice, and roaches in the building sneaking out at the worst possible time. I killed one of the bats with a tennis racket once. Little pieces of ceiling fell into my coffee cup in the morning, but I drank it anyway and moved on. I was here and I was going to make the best of it.

I was given a budget of $500 a month to hire one assistant who could help me recruit the first prospective players. I brought in one of my former players who had just graduated from college and wanted to get into coaching. We went everywhere that spring and summer and brought in a total of forty-three new students. Of these maybe a handful were potential football players.

We knew we were going to have slim pickings at that time of the year. Coupled with the fact that our program was so new it didn't even exist yet football players weren't as anxious to come on board. Many of them had other options at schools with well-established programs.

So we looked for qualities and raw talent. If the young men we found had the right attitude and skill set I knew we could transform that into a football team.

It took a few months to figure out how the team was going to be administered and conducted. The University had announced they hired me as their first football coach in March, but it took until October to hammer out the particulars. I wasn't really a coach yet—I had nothing and no one to coach. I was more of a consultant. But both the university and I had to take a leap of faith and believe it would all work out.

We measured our progress in baby steps. I moved from the condemned dorm to an old shack. It was a step up and every move that we made brought us closer to having a real team.

I brought in Mike Ward who had been with me at Georgetown, but he was doubtful I could pull it off. He cast a skeptical glance at the less-than-stellar setup, and said, "I'm just not seeing the vision."

I hired Warren Maloney as defensive coordinator and persuaded Dave Ivy to volunteer as an assistant. It took some doing because no one was quite sure it was going to work out, least of all me. But there was something about Saint Francis- almost an aura of sorts that kept me focused. Maybe it was that both the University and I were at all-time lows. We somehow found each other at just the right time. I look back now and can see God's hand at work bringing me to Saint Francis and surrounding me with just the right people.

All I needed to do was find just the right players. On top of that we needed to increase enrollment, which would provide more tuition money to support the school. My assistant and I were out trying to sell a program that didn't yet exist, and to join a team that wouldn't even have helmets until the following year.

We also didn't have scholarship money to offer them. The reality is, most student athletes don't go to school on scholarship. The stats from the NAIA (National Association of Intercollegiate Athletics) show that even a school's top players are often paying for school. But we were offering almost nothing—and hoping for everything from these guys.

At first the school only wanted twenty recruits. I knew I needed more than that especially because many of them wouldn't be football players. We had to recruit more so we had more options for positions.

Those forty-three we recruited were a motley group, but they were moldable, teachable, and most of all, enthusiastic. That first spring practice in April of 1998 was a disaster. We were so bad that if we had played the nuns they would have been a two-touchdown favorite. We were so pathetic we couldn't have beaten anyone, but we had some pretty good kids coming into that freshman class. We had a kid who could throw the ball, a kid who could catch it, and a few who were competitive on the line of scrimmage.

My very first task I had to turn around the kids' self-image. It was so bad they even made fun of themselves. They thought and believed they were a joke. We worked hard trying to instill dignity, self-confidence, and build a sense of pride. I needed and wanted them to believe in themselves as much as I believed in what we were doing.

I went into the recruitment meetings and practices with one consistent message: This is who we are, this is what we are all about, and this is the tradition we are going to build.

When I'm coaching players my number one goal is to teach these young people to be the best they can be: to be productive citizens in our society, and to be responsible and accountable for their actions. That's what creates a successful football program more than drills and practice games. Attitude and commitment can shoot a mediocre team into greatness. These young men had what it took—all we needed was the infrastructure and the practice to bring it out of them and through that create a team: a team that would make everyone proud—me, the university, the community, and most important of all, the players.

PART TWO

GAME TIME

Chapter 7

The 1998 'Test' Season

I had players. But what I needed just as much was money.

At Saint Francis the blank slate meant I wasn't starting with the negativity I'd found in my previous jobs. There was no 'win at all costs' attitude. But there was a constant argument about institutional funding and endless discussion of how an intercollegiate football program would be run. The essential question was what percentage of tuition income would be used to fund a scholarship base within NAIA rules and how much of that money would be used for an operating budget to buy equipment, cover travel costs, hire a coaching staff, and other things.

Some in the university hierarchy thought starting a football program was an unwise decision. For the university it meant a four-year investment with no real financial return in terms of tuition. Even if there had been an immediate ROI (Return on Investment) there were still massive up-front expenditures to be made. We needed facilities—locker rooms, a field, stadium, and equipment. Saint Francis needed to either borrow money and pay it back on a four-year basis or raise the funding they needed. It was a daunting challenge.

For me this meant becoming a part of Fort Wayne. I had to make connections and build relationships with those who wished to get involved. One of the first people I met was Doug McKibben. He introduced me to Tom Jehl, Jim Shields, and John Tippmann. Most were long-time Notre Dame season ticket holders. When they heard we were creating a football team right there in Fort Wayne they got involved and contributed.

The result was the building of a $2.1 million stadium with locker rooms and a training facility. It was bare bones, but nice for its time. Half of the funding came from those guys getting involved and the rest was drawn from tuition income.

The support of these generous private benefactors meant the university didn't have to pay back that tuition money over four years. It freed up funds to hire a sports marketing director, which meant we could get our games on the air. Having a sports marketing director then opened doors to advertising, corporate donations, and private gifts.

Things were looking brighter, but the Promised Land was still off in the distance and down a long winding, bumpy, and difficult road filled with potholes and hazards of many different kinds. Saint Francis football was an unproven commodity working on achieving a dream.

That went for the team as well. We had this fantastic stadium, but before that our first locker room was the back of a semi-truck trailer. In the spring of 1998 we handed out the first box of equipment—shoulder pads and helmets. Helmets don't come with facemasks already on them and I knew we were in trouble when one of the kids said, "Coach this helmet don't fit." I looked at him and realized he had the helmet on backwards. I took it off, turned it around, slapped it back on his head and sent him on his way.

Those forty-three players were pretty inexperienced. They were red-shirted which meant they were in school but didn't participate in competition. The second recruiting class that started in the fall of 1998 was an improvement. Nevertheless Saint Francis had about ninety-six potential players—none of whom had ever played in a college football game.

That inaugural season was a learning experience for everyone. We won two games, but didn't win at home. You just lick your wounds, keep on truckin', and get through it.

Like any fledgling venture to get the advertising dollars and the support people had to believe in the cause and see the big picture. I met with donor after donor trying to get them to see my dream. I was enthusiastic and excited and I think it showed. I believed the University of Saint Francis would win a national title someday. I was confident the Cougars would play for a national title within ten years. It was a bold promise that seemed more like wishful thinking and I'm sure a lot of people thought I was crazy.

It only took me six years, but I delivered on that promise.

There were a lot of hurdles to jump between those first practices and a championship though. After over a year of preparation trying to turn a rag-tag bunch of kids into college football players we were ready to play real college football. Our first game was against Saint Xavier University in Chicago.

The Friday before we left I sat them down and talked to them about the trip—the schedule, mealtimes, meetings, and the importance of being on time. Most of these players had never been out of Fort Wayne or Allen County and now they were about to go on an overnight trip to Chicago and stay in a hotel. Half of them had never even stayed in a hotel before.

I wanted them to understand this was a business trip not a vacation. We were going up there to win a game. I finished my lecture and asked if there were any questions. I saw a hand go up. "Coach can we take our swim trunks?" one of the kids asked. All I could do was laugh.

The bus trip was a lot like going to Gilligan's Island. Our three-hour trip ended up taking eight hours. We were riding up there in two beat-up charter buses. The seats in one of the buses kept falling apart. The bus carrying the defensive unit had seats that would just fall out. Then one of the drivers took a detour because he wanted to stop at the gambling casino in Michigan City.

One driver didn't speak English and the other had a serious attitude problem. After the casino detour the two buses somehow got separated. I knew St. Xavier University was on the south side of Chicago. When I saw a sign announcing we were two miles from the Wisconsin State Line I knew we were going in the wrong direction. I told the driver, but he just ignored me and kept going.

I yelled at him and he got really angry and stopped right in the middle of an expressway off-ramp and threw a tantrum. He throws the bus in park and gets off. He didn't want me telling him how to drive the bus and refused to admit he was going the wrong way. He was ready to square off against me but the other coaches got involved and eventually we talked him down, got him back on the bus, and turned around.

We had departed from Fort Wayne about 3 o'clock in the afternoon but our bus didn't pull into the hotel until 10:30 p.m. that night. We were so late that the dinner the hotel had prepared was cold. The second bus didn't pull in until about midnight. They had gotten lost in Chicago's Little Mexico and had been driving around trying to get directions, but no one on the bus could speak Spanish. All the players were in bed after one in the morning after a dinner of cold chicken and pasta.

However the adventure wasn't over. The next morning we somehow got lost between the hotel and the field. The hotel was a mile away from Saint Xavier, but the drivers still somehow got turned around. We arrived at the stadium about an hour before kickoff, which is an hour later than I like to arrive for an away game. We got off the bus and we're throwing equipment on, taping kids, and lining up to play. We barely had enough time to run through our pregame warm up.

Saint Xavier kicked off. Saint Francis went down and scored on the first series, and at halftime, we led 28-7. We ended up winning our first football game 56-28, even though we barely had a clue. Maybe the fact that we had close to three hundred nuns praying for us that day played a part.

That was the high for that season. We lost our next seven games before we won again, a win that was a total act of God.

Throughout our first season, Saint Francis got spanked hard. In one game, we were down 40-0 at halftime. I pulled the other coaches aside and said we had to do something. It was embarrassing and I was worried one of our players would get hurt—that's how strong this other team was. I went into the locker room and said to the team, "You people either have to get out there and fight your tail off and give your best or get on that bus and go back to Fort Wayne."

Someone asked, "Coach can we do that?" I laughed. Still those boys went back out there and gave it all they had.

In another game we played at Tri-State (now Trine University), we were in trouble before we even started. Tri-State was undefeated and went all the way to the NAIA semi-finals that year. Early in the second half Tri-State stopped us deep in our own territory. We were in a fourth down and nineteen situation as we prepared to punt from about our own 20-yard line, but instead of punting our kicker took the snap and ran with it. He dove toward the yard marker thinking he was at the first down stick mark, but he wasn't. He had another ten yards to go.

Tri-State turned that mistake into a score and our game just fell apart. The final score was 71-27. We struggled through that first year won a couple games and lost a lot more than that. I just thank God we didn't get anybody killed. That's how the football program at Saint Francis started.

That first year was a battle on many levels. Not just in forming a team, but in creating strong player-coach relationships while also building rapport with the administration and community. The important thing was making sure everyone saw day-to-day progress.

Once the program was up and running and the kids felt good about what they were doing it was a matter of keeping that positive attitude and staying on top of the players to be sure they were making good decisions. Young men face many temptations in college. They're under a lot of pressure from their instructors, their coaches, and their families. Many come in with troubled histories and baggage.

To be part of that process of helping young men grow into great adults is the rewarding part of coaching. Even when changes are for the better and will make their long-term prospects brighter some people resist those changes. It takes more than a single conversation to direct and teach them.

Many of the incoming freshmen resented the rules and structure. They didn't like having to curtail partying or concentrate on grades. They fought me on drug testing and said it was an invasion of their privacy. The players simply didn't grasp the meaning of being responsible to more than themselves. I had to help them see that they were part of something bigger.

Our student athletes, especially the ones on scholarship are essentially employees. It's our responsibility to teach them they are always going to have a boss. Even if you own your own business you still aren't free of having to be accountable. Adults abide by laws, pay taxes, and work with other people. I want my athletes to learn that life is about doing the right things, being straight up with other people, putting the curbs on the table, and learning to agree to disagree.

Starting a program from scratch gave me more room to build this character within my athletes, the team and the program overall. I figured if I could lay a strong foundation that could weather the inevitable storms that would come up the football program would grow and flourish. That was my prayer in that inaugural year—sometimes a prayer I made several times a day because even I had my moments of doubt.

Chapter 8

Worst to First

The 1999 Season

University of Saint Francis
1999 Cougars

Until Saint Francis won the National Championship in 2016 when you walked into the door of the football office underneath Bishop D'Arcy Stadium you would see an eight by ten foot picture of the 1999 Cougars in the hallway. That team, that year, has a special place in my heart and memory. The picture is no longer in that hallway, but it is still on display in a different location.

We ended the 1998 season with a 2-8 record. I knew we needed to make changes to improve our prospects in 1999.

That spring the first order of business was to have a team meeting. The previous fall we'd been in such a rush to cobble together a team and get them out on the field that we hadn't had time to establish who the Cougars were, what our goals were, and what our team was trying to do. They divided the problem into parts. First they had to establish purpose. What were they there for? Was it just to win football games? They worked hard on answering the question 'Why are we here?'

The answers to these questions were important in more than one way. I was well aware the president of the university had stuck her neck out to start a college football program when it wasn't exactly a popular decision. I was committed to making sure we were building our team on a solid foundation. A foundation that represented the University of Saint Francis in a first-class manner with football players who were going to be role models for the other students on the campus and the citizens of Fort Wayne who were watching the program get off the ground.

The 1999 season began with us losing our best running back. He opted not to return to USF and we started hunting for a replacement right away. We got lucky—the replacement was bigger, stronger, and better equipped to help the Cougars reach their goals.

The young team matured a lot from year one to year two. Not only were they a year older, but they also had more focus, different attitudes, team chemistry, and started exhibiting more shear enjoyment for the game. They worked hard every day and Saturday, game day, was the party.

They started creating their own traditions and chants. Some of those traditions, especially the goofy pregame warm-up fun have stayed to this day. I was happy to let the team have a hand in what made us the Cougars and to carry forward what those early teams started. They projected their own persona of what traditions are all about and what this team meant to them.

The 1999 team was filled with young people who accepted responsibility and were accountable. By far, they were one of the greatest groups I've ever coached. Maybe it was because they were overachievers (much like my 1991 national title team at Georgetown), or maybe it was because they learned to overcome so much.

In the early years of the program between 1999 and 2005 we practiced on a small 60-yard field on the southeast corner of Lindenwood Avenue and Bass Road. It was all that was available within a reasonable distance not to mention affordable. Earlier it had been the location of an old storage barn and even though I had the field leveled it was far from perfect. Practicing there was like trying to navigate an obstacle course. The torn-down building foundation was still there, and the players were dodging rocks and building debris or running into the old fences that surrounded the property.

The kids sometimes complained, but I kept reminding them every adverse circumstance was an opportunity. It didn't matter whether you practiced on rocks, avoided cars, or came up against a formidable opponent; it was an opportunity to show yourself, your coach, and your team what you were made of.

I want these young men to see adversity as opportunity. We're a glass half-full kind of team. We do the right things, we give it our best shot, and above all, we always maintain a positive attitude. Don't complain about the disagreeable and difficult circumstances—attack them with optimism.

Those nervous freshmen in 1998 matured and developed into much better players in 1999. Even though they only had two wins their first season they had a real desire to do better. That transformation began to show itself in January in the weight room. We'd converted an old storage room in the gym into the weight room and we'd cobbled together whatever we could for equipment. But the kids worked out there without complaint and worked out hard.

We were blessed with a good quarterback and a good receiver on offense along with several good linemen. One of those linemen from the 1999 team went on to become an ultimate fighter. He was a tough kid, jovial, and likable, raised in a juvenile detention center. He kind of latched on to me like a dad. Even though it seemed like we were taking anybody who had a pulse, we ended up getting some fabulous players.

That year, Saint Francis joined the Mid-States Football Association a group that included a number of highly regarded NAIA football programs. In the fall of 1999 Saint Francis was picked to finish last in the league's Eastern Division. To everyone's surprise, they ended up finishing first.

A lot of that first-place strength happened over the winter and spring. It was in the attitude, the hard work, the practices, and the traditions that began to turn this rag-tag bunch into a true team. We won some games against teams that on paper at least we should not have won.

Although it didn't seem that way at first, the beginning of season two looked a lot like a continuation of season one. Saint Francis traveled to Valparaiso University for their first game. Valparaiso was division 1A and had played Yale the week before. They beat the tar out of us and I thought we were just going to repeat the year before.

The next week the Cougars played McKendree University a well-regarded NAIA team and experienced more of the same. Although we lost it was by a slimmer margin.

With a 0-2 start, Saint Francis played Saint Xavier next in a home game. The two teams were pretty equally matched and heading into the third quarter we had a two-touchdown lead. St. Xavier scored, but we were driving and inside the ten-yard line. Our quarterback fumbled the ball, and their defense picked it up and it ran back ninety yards for the score. They lined up to go for two and took the lead.

I pulled our quarterback aside. He was in tears because he fumbled the ball. But the play was over and it was time to move on. I looked him straight in the eye and said, "It's time for you to grow up right now. You are going to grow up in the next thirty-eight seconds we have left. Now get down there and work the two-minute drill and win this game!"

This moment even though I didn't realize it at the time was the crucial turnaround of the season. Young teams sometimes give away a game. The quarterback was on the brink of that. But instead of wallowing in his mistake he became the spark and the glue that pulled it together. Saint Francis had a great receiver on that team and he and the quarterback worked one-on-one all the way down the field and we won the game right at the end. After that win, our confidence zoomed. We snowballed off that.

The next week Saint Francis traveled to Tiffin University in Tiffin, Ohio. Tiffin was our first conference game. Tiffin was ranked, undefeated, and the top pick of the league. They had athletes, including Nate Washington who later played for the Pittsburgh Steelers. They tried to intimidate us because they were confident that they had what it took and we didn't.

Apparently the young team from Saint Francis missed the memo from Tiffin. All their taunts lit a fire in the Cougars. Our guys fought Tiffin tooth and nail all afternoon. Saint Francis led by two or three points but Tiffin was driving. The Cougars had a 5'5" 160-pound free safety named Will Barnes who stepped up and picked off a pass from Tiffin. He grabbed that ball, ran for the touchdown and Saint Francis won.

Coupled with the come-from-behind-win the week before Saint Francis was on a roll. The Cougars were now 1-0 in the conference and 2-2 overall. Beating Tiffin was an electrical charge for the team. Every practice became fun. The kids had smiles on their faces, the other coaches were laughing, but still we played with intensity.

Saint Francis won seven straight victories before facing Walsh University to determine the conference championship. Walsh was undefeated in conference play as were we. Because we had beat Tiffin, that put us at the top of the league against a very tough team.

Walsh is located in Canton, Ohio home of the Pro Football Hall of Fame. It was the first time the Cougars played on the Pro Football Hall of Fame field where both Walsh and Malone University, another league member, played their home games. Walsh was bigger, faster, and better, at least on paper, but Saint Francis was full of heart and optimism.

Saint Francis took charge that day. Our offense was unstoppable and we had an advantage in our passing game. No matter what Walsh tried Saint Francis was able to position well enough to cover and block them from scoring too many points.

We won. I was just as stunned as the players. Here we were, on a field where football greats had played and we were the winners. It was an unbelievable day. Art Mandelbomb, who was a local attorney, had championship hats made up and waiting for us on the sidelines. That was the only hat I wore for many years.

In 1999 Saint Francis finished undefeated in conference and with an 8-2 record overall. In just our second season we found ourselves in the playoffs—ironically playing against Georgetown. It was a bittersweet moment when we lost to the school I had been working at just a few years prior. Nevertheless I was incredibly proud of the team. We had gone from 2-8 to 8-2 in one year with essentially the same team of players.

***

My own plate was fuller in 1999. The previous Athletic Director resigned and took a high school job in Cincinnati. Rather than hiring someone new the school president called me and said, "You're the Athletic Director."

That gave me a peek inside the other athletic program at Saint Francis, which gave me a better view of where football fit and how to make the program grow. The basketball program was also a little anemic. They had about three scholarships and their coaches were underpaid. I went to work on getting them fully funded. I knew that in a community like Fort Wayne basketball and football would be the most visible in the media and thus gain more community support. I wanted to create a greater awareness of the university, which would lead to increased enrollment.

It worked. Admissions at Saint Francis doubled within two years and then kept on growing and growing, and today total enrollment stands at the 2,500 mark. Football wasn't the only draw—sometimes you recruit a football player and a buddy or a girlfriend will follow. Or students hear about the great athletics program and realize Saint Francis has a stellar academics program too. There's also word of mouth—our students are proud to talk about how much they love this school.

Many of the guys we recruited early in the program came, studied, played, left, and then spread the word about Saint Francis. They've become essential in recruiting and bringing kids in and because they are such enthusiastic supporters they have helped make recruiting easier.

I credit a lot of this to that 1999 Cougar football team. They changed the tone for all the teams to come. In 2008, they were inducted into the University of Saint Francis Hall of Fame. I look at the picture and realize all of the guys in that photo were on that first bus trip. It's still incredible to think we went from worst to first in a matter of eight months.

How did that happen? They were picked for last. They weren't very good yet. The second recruiting class arrived and filled a few holes from the year before, but it was still essentially that same team we had red-shirted. I think we had a number of things fall into place at the same time. We won a few games we shouldn't have won. We played hard in some close contests and prevailed. That time in the weight room in January helped the guys' focus on the mental part of the game as well as getting stronger and doing things together as a team. They formed a real bond, a unity on and off the field.

We also built a good coach/player relationship with all of the coaching staff. The team had fun with the coaches and the coaches liked each other. No one ever said a bad word about another person, a pretty remarkable feat for an organization encompassing more than a hundred different and diverse personalities.

What that created was harmony on the field. We fought the wars as a unit. Offense won games. Defense won games. We won games together.

Confidence, coming together as a group, and everybody taking ownership to the whole operation were the biggest factors in that 1999 team going from worst to first. So much of football is a mental game. When you start erasing doubt and you start thinking *we can* instead of *we can't* – whatever you believe is usually true. Of course a little luck and having the ball bounce in the right direction doesn't hurt.

That 1999 season was the start of something good. From the start, I swear everyone could tell it was going to be something special. It was like an aura that was building. There was a swagger, a confidence, kind of like what Notre Dame used to have, about our team. We believed we could do it—and we did.

***

Saint Francis's remarkable turnaround and achievements in 1999 changed everything. All of a sudden the advertising opened up and the corporate sector got involved with the private sector. All the networking I had done in the past began to pay off.

Privately and corporately enthusiasm for the team just grew, grew and grew. Maybe because we had been the underdogs, the ones people loved to hold up as an example of conquering the impossible.

The sudden success on the field had other beneficial effects. Our recruitment circle got wider and we were able to build a Northeast Indiana all-star team that showcased a lot of local talent and helped build awareness and support.

We also began having "honorary coaches" for the day. The CEO of Steel Dynamics, for example got to come out on the sidelines and call a few plays in the fourth quarter. Daniel Ruettiger, whose own story was the basis of the movie *Rudy* and a country western star appeared at games. They were friends of friends who came to lend support, and their appearances didn't cost anything. It was free publicity.

***

The local business people began to step up too. One company offered to make a $2.5 million donation. A prominent local banker and community leader got involved supporting the health science programs at the university. Another retired CEO) and long-time community leader became a part of promoting the arts at Saint Francis. A Fort Wayne developer went to Eli Lily and convinced them to match all the contributions, which took that original $2.5 million donation and ballooned it to $10 million. The goodwill in the Fort Wayne community built more every day. After a long period in the rain the sun was beginning to shine brightly on the University of Saint Francis.

Each one of these moves spurred another one like branches of a tree spreading and interconnecting. A long-time member of the Saint Francis Board of Trustees purchased a church property adjacent to the university to give the university a place for convocations, meetings, offices, parking, and other needed facilities. A local entrepreneur purchased thirty acres of land west of Lindenwood Avenue and to the west of the football complex for future development of the athletic fields and other uses. As of this writing, that land is being readied for development to accommodate future soccer, baseball, softball, and track teams. That means the current fields will be available for future classrooms and other purposes.

Suddenly the University of Saint Francis which only a short time before had been at the edge of extinction not sure it could make its next payroll had many of Fort Wayne's heavy hitters providing support. They were involved in the university and the dream and many of them can now be seen on Saturday afternoons in the fall cheering the Cougars from the sidelines while watching the team notch another victory.

Some things took a little more time to become fruitful. That's how it was with the Cougars. We planted a lot of seeds in those early years that took time to bud, flower, and then become roots in the program. When I first started at Saint Francis, I was invited to appear on local radio sports talk show hosted by a guy named Lefty Davis, Phil Houk and Art Mandelbaum. The three of them weren't naysayers, they were supportive, knew I had a strong coaching history, and kept an eye on our progress. I kept in touch with the three of them, and when we wanted to air our games, Houk and Mandelbaum became part of the broadcast team.

Those small connections became roots for much bigger ones down the road. Houk and Jeff Leffers, who was then Director of Court Operations, Allen Superior Court, went out and spoke to community associations about the football program. They were excited about what they were seeing, and their support helped spread the word.

In the fall of 1997 a year before Saint Francis was scheduled to begin playing, I appeared on another talk show. I thought I'd have the whole hour to tout what we were doing at Saint Francis, but the host had me on with Lifetime Sports Academy Director Tom Jehl. Tom was a proponent of getting kids out to play golf and tennis, and he didn't have a lot of faith that Saint Francis would ever play a game of football. It wasn't the most auspicious first meeting.

But the next February Jehl showed up at my office and asked, "What can I do to help?" He was impressed with what we had accomplished and how we had gotten the program off the ground. He jumped right in and helped finance us then went on to introduce me to other people in the community who were interested in lending a helping hand. That one door led to a lot of other opened doors.

The Lifetime Sports Academy started at the same time as our football program. Jehl's goal was to take troubled kids and give them a new perspective and outlook on life. The program was designed to not only give the participants sports skills, but also provide them with a productive outlet. In turn that would help reduce the crime rate increase participation in sports across the city and help create stronger more well rounded teens.

In the beginning, Jehl used a lot of his own money and worked in cooperation and support of the Fort Wayne Park and Recreation Department. Today the program has more than 2,000 kids participating each summer. Its impact on the community has changed people's lives and trickled down to improve university enrollment. Over the years, he and I worked together to establish several sports scholarships. After Jehl died two four-year scholarships were created, one for a male and one for a female graduate of the Lifetime Sports Academy. This was a way for the university and the community to embrace each other and to change the lives of kids who wouldn't otherwise have the opportunity to attend college.

Since I started working at Saint Francis university enrollment has gone up five-fold. That's due to a lot of factors— increased donations, increased sports success, and increased media exposure. The city of Fort Wayne is also a major component of that success. For every one person who comes up and says something negative about our program, I get five hundred others who come up and say, "I really appreciate what you are doing for this community."

***

Success, I have found, is about people and relationships both on and off the field. Fort Wayne has that secret combination, and that has been a big part of elevating Saint Francis to where it is today. A different city might not have had the same result. I was at Georgetown College in Kentucky for eleven years and won a national title in 1991. While I was there I built teams that scored the most points of any team in the 20th century—59.5 points a game, 744 points overall—and yet I could never get the community, businesses, business leaders, or anybody else to become more involved in that program until after the school won a national championship. In contrast, Fort Wayne community support was there before we ever played a game.

Part of it might be because Georgetown's program had been around forever and had never done very well. At Saint Francis there were no preconceived ideas other than a few cynics and naysayers who didn't think we'd be able to make it. I think it was easier to build from scratch rather than trying to overcome an existing program that was consistently losing on the field.

In a few short years our football program accomplished more than many programs that have been around forever. That built goodwill quickly and created incentive for local players to choose Saint Francis after high school. We recruited a number of good players from local and high schools because the kids there wanted to join our team.

As part of our community involvement and outreach we opened use of our stadium and facilities to the Fort Wayne CYO. They play their games on Saint Francis's field on Sundays. For these fifth and sixth graders simply playing in Bishop D'Arcy stadium is a huge deal and honor. It's exciting to see these young kids start on our field, graduate from high school and then enroll at Saint Francis for college. High school coaches come to watch, the Catholic bishop and priests come, and in turn, these Sunday games create family growth and bonding throughout the Catholic community.

***

Not every sponsor said yes and not every meeting resulted in support. But eventually, most people came around as they saw our success grow. A local pizza franchise wanted nothing to do with us when I first approached them for sponsorship. But three years later after we started winning on the field the franchise owner came up to me and regretted not being our pizza sponsor.

So much of the success of Saint Francis in the community was a team effort—and I mean the team outside of the Cougars. People who were behind us went out and talked about the program, brought their friends and peers into the circle, and began to build the word of mouth that is so valuable in getting anything off the ground. The unselfish efforts of many generous benefactors in the Fort Wayne community has helped put the football program, and more importantly the university, on solid footing that will help it continue growing long into the future.

Chapter 9

Building on the Foundation of Success

In 2000 the Cougars finished 9-1 and recorded their first playoff victory against Lambuth University. Saint Francis had the same quarterback and receiver combination from 1999 and fielded a very strong passing team. They had the same basic group on defense. It was no surprise they had a great year even though they ended up losing in the quarterfinals to the eventual national champion—Georgetown. My former assistant coach, Bill Cronin, is the coach there now. We can be bitter enemies for four hours on the field, but as soon as the game is over we're friends again. I respect what he's done with the

Georgetown program something that was clear in that 2000 game. They played hard and deserved that win. Although our boys were disappointed it was clear 2000 was a year of success—success made possible by the strong foundation we already had established in the past two seasons

The 2001 Season

In 2001 Saint Francis had high aspirations. We had won a couple of conference championships and expected big things. This was our program's fourth season. We had twenty-four seniors—our first senior class. We had lost our principal receiver Jeremy Dutcher when he graduated, and try as we might, we couldn't get it together on a consistent basis. The chemistry simply wasn't there. We'd had success the second and third year, but just couldn't pull off the same thing in 2001.

The first part of the season was great—we were undefeated and ranked in the top five in the country going into our ninth game. This was the most critical game of the season because it was a conference champion deciding game.

Just before that game I found out eight seniors had broken team rules including our quarterback, who was the leading passer in the country. The timing couldn't have been worse. This conference title would top our first undefeated season and give us a high seeding position in the upcoming playoffs. It would have been understandable and easy for me to turn my back and look the other way, but that would mean compromising everything I believed in and everything I was trying to teach these young men.

I couldn't turn around and make a decision that broke the very principles I lived my life by. I suspended those eight seniors knowing the cost. The eight backups I brought in did their best, but Tri-State beat us on the last play of the game. We finished the regular season 9-1.

I don't regret doing the right thing. It was a learning experience for the players and for this program. The players are always looking to the coach to lead—to make those tough decisions, because it sends a message about what our team is really about. It's not about winning it's about living a life you can be proud of, a life built on strong principles.

2001 was a year I had anticipated as the year we could make a run for the national title but that didn't happen. Even after that loss Saint Francis was still ranked in the top eight. We ended losing in the quarterfinals at Campbellsville, KY 42-21. We finished the year with a 9-2 record. It was disappointing but doing the right thing was more important.

The 2002 Season

In 2002 the Cougars started the next generation of players. We graduated eighteen starters at the end of 2001, but we had a strong freshman group both in offense and defense. 2001 was our first undefeated 10-0 regular season. I had some truly standout players that year like receiver Andy Papagiannis who was 5'8" 150 pounds and could run the forty in five seconds flat. He had such heart and serious enthusiasm.

It was Cory Jacquay's first year, and this starter ended up becoming national player of the year. Other kids like Adam Denning and Antoine Taylor just brought good energy to the group. The entire team played with such excitement that year.

1999 was an unbelievable year, 2000 was a good year, 2001 was expected to be great, but turned out to be a learning year, and then 2002 came. It was as if everything we had been working on suddenly aligned. Even though we lost in the quarterfinals of the NAIA playoffs to Georgetown (who went on to become national champions), that year of Cougar football was absolutely incredible.

Chapter 10

Coming Close

The 2003 Season

That year set the tone going forward. Over the next six years we had an incredible run. We finished the regular season undefeated from 2002 through 2006 before losing to our conference rival Ohio Dominican in 2007.

In 2003 we reached the final four before losing at Carroll College in Helena, Montana. In 2004, 2005, and 2006 the Cougars reached the NAIA Championship game before losing to Carroll College twice, and the University of Sioux Falls (South Dakota). It was a series of really great years with some amazing teamwork.

Part of the difference during those four years was Chris Bramell. He was a 6-6, 240-pound kid everybody wanted to recruit as a tight end but I saw a quarterback in him. Bramell was a tough competitor. He was a physical kid and would just plow forward; running over people doing whatever it took to get to where he was going. He wasn't a phenomenal passer but he had a great presence and Saint Francis was a different type of team during his years here.

Our season opener in 2003 was against Tiffin. Tiffin had dropped out of the Mid-States Conference of NAIA schools and moved to play in NCAA Division II. Their big receiver (who later played with the Pittsburgh Stealers) was still there. They were big, nasty, and tough. And I'm not going to lie, a little intimidating.

We were on our own home turf with everyone in the stands expecting an incredible opening game. At one point we had a fourth down and three at our own 35-yard line. We were down ten points so we decided to gamble and go for it. We ran a naked boot with Bramell, our quarterback. We had a great play fake that worked—everybody jumped on Luther Stroder and tackled him while Bramell was running sixty-five yards for the touchdown. That moment ignited our team and got Bramell off to an illustrious three years.

Later in that same game we were stalled deep in our own territory inside the 10. Tiffin was ready for our fake play this time, but Bramell blew through three tackles and made another touchdown. Unfortunately there was a penalty on the play and it nullified the play. Nevertheless that game was incredible and a great way to start that season.

Also in 2003 we had one of the craziest finishes I've ever seen in a college football game. We were playing a home game against Saint Ambrose who was ranked number three just ahead of us at number four. The game was close and the score kept going back and forth, back and forth. The Cougars led 12-7 the first quarter, then 25-14 at the half. Saint Ambrose scored 19 points in the fourth quarter and took a 41-39 lead with about 30 seconds left on the clock.

Saint Francis responded. The team did what they'd been taught on the practice field. They went into their two-minute drill, completed a couple passes, before our receiver broke a tackle and drove the ball all the way to the three-yard line. With only two seconds on the clock I called for a time out. I tell the guys to go for a field goal. I look down at the north-west corner of the end zone and I see Sister Elise on her knees praying.

We attempted to kick the field goal and it was blocked. This is where a well-trained team can pull it together while a badly trained team can fall apart. The ball came back to the kicker Clint Bontempo and Andy Papagiannis yells "Fire! Fire!"

They work the drill in reverse as Clint rolls out to the left and pitches it to Andy who runs it in scoring a touchdown and winning the game. Saint Ambrose had gotten cocky and sure about their victory after they blocked that kick so they took their eyes off of Clint and Andy. When Andy scored that touchdown the Cougar fans went wild. Fans jumped over the fences, Sister Elise got drenched in beer, and everyone went wild. We won because those two kids knew what to do. The whole team didn't quit and found a way to win no matter the odds.

Years later, I was at a roast honoring University of Saint Francis President Sister Elise. I told that story about that Saint Ambrose game. She said she hadn't liked my decision to kick a field goal so that's why she started praying at the goal line. I laughed and told her if she had told me we would have run a play.

By the time of the 2003 Championship Playoffs the Cougars were a top ten team in the NAIA. In the playoffs against Georgetown things looked bleak once again. We were down 16-14 going into the fourth quarter. Georgetown had beaten us at this critical juncture two times before but not this time. Our team came out from behind poured on the steam and scored 20 points to win 34-23.

The quarterfinal round was a rematch with Saint Ambrose and the Bees were still stirred up after losing in our first match in what they called 'a fluke.' The game was a home game on Saint Francis's still rudimentary turf field. It was before we put down the synthetic surface and that meant we were playing in muddy thick earth. You could have planted corn after the game the soil was so rich and thick.

Rain was in the weather forecast so after the walk-through on Friday afternoon, we called in everybody—coaches and players—and laid tarps out to cover the field. Indiana weather can be unpredictable, especially in November, and when we got up next morning the rain had turned out to be eight inches of snow.

The game was scheduled for a noon kick off time. We had to get the tarps off the field, but temperatures fell so fast that when the rain turned to snow the tarps had frozen to the ground. I got my team in there and set them to work removing snow. Took us three hours and we ended up moving the start time back two hours to 2 pm.

When Saint Ambrose arrived they were overjoyed to see us expending our pre-game energy removing snow and tarps. I didn't say it at the time but I was pretty worried our kids were going to be physically exhausted and it would affect their game.

But I'd forgotten these guys were Saint Francis Cougars. They shoveled snow from nine in the morning to about a quarter of one, went in, got dressed, and went back out on the field and played a hell of a game. We were 13-7 at the halftime break and then we went on to score 28 more points in the second half. We just went out there and shellacked them. Adversity, as I had told my team more than once, is opportunity. We proved that with a final score of 41-14.

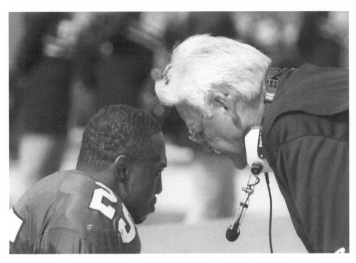

Facing and overcoming adversity is an inescapable
part of life. Donley uses every moment to teach.

We lost to Carroll College in Helena, Montana in the
semi-finals the next week but overall, 2003 had been a great
year. We had finally hit our groove, and the next few seasons
were all about perfecting that synergy.

The 2004 Season

2004 was almost a repeat of 2003. We finished the regular
season 10-0, and 7-0 in the Mid-States Conference Eastern
Division. In the playoffs we breezed past Morningside 53-3
and Hastings 48-17 before we earned a contested 12-7 win
over Georgetown in the semi-finals. Two weeks later we found

ourselves playing Carroll College again but this time for the National Championship.

The NAIA championship game was at Jim Carroll Stadium in Savannah, Tennessee. The game was close and low scoring. We scored late in the fourth quarter to take a slim lead with about a minute and a half remaining. Then Carroll got the ball back, went into their two-minute drill, made a couple passes, and got down to the fifteen-yard line. Carroll hadn't moved the ball against our Cougar defense all day. Now they sent their field goal team out with about 10 seconds left. The snap from center was high and the guy receiving the snap jumped up, caught it, and spiked the ball. Spiking the ball wasn't allowed under NAIA rules in that situation but the ref didn't rule against it so consequently Carroll got a second chance and nailed it for the win.

It just goes to show how quickly things can turn and change. I had learned that lesson on the plane earlier that summer and that moment had me rethinking my priorities where my life was going and what I wanted out of this time. It was about much more than just winning and hitting the national level.

Still it's always a little tough to swallow a loss. I thought we had outplayed Carroll that day. Both defenses were great that year and I knew going in that it would be a low scoring game. But in the end just as we had in the game against Saint Ambrose Carroll pulled off a last-minute miracle.

2004 was the Cougars' first of three consecutive appearances in the NAIA championships in Savannah, Tennessee. Our strong defensive game was due in part to Brian Kurtz. 2004 was his sophomore year and over the next three years he gave the defense an aggressive attacking quality. He was tough and aggressive the perfect combination for a defensive linebacker. He was responsible for a whole lot of our defensive tenacity in 2004, 2005, and 2006. He could be a pain in the ass at times and drove Defensive Coordinator Warren Maloney nuts. But I kind of like a kid with a little challenge to him and that was Kurtz.

We also had a great offensive line in those years. They were a dominating group, strong, very efficient. After they left it wasn't quite the same at least for some time. Linebacker Joey Didier, now the Cougar's Defensive Co-coordinator, won Saint Francis's coveted silver helmet award. He was a great kid, always did the right thing, and did whatever it took to get the task done.

Then we had Bramell, the tight end converted to quarterback, who provided Saint Francis's offense with the same kind of toughness Kurtz provided to the defense.

In those years we had a great group of young men on the team. They had character, strength, and fortitude. It's hard to find a senior class that can always stay focused on the game. Their gazes are on what's to come—careers, family, living on their own. School is nearly over and in their heads it's often already in the rearview mirror. But that 2002 team had a lot of heart and excitement two things that carried forward through 2006.

Couple all that with a positive attitude and you generate that vital magic and electricity that makes up a winning team.

The 2005 Season

The 2005 season started a little different from other years. Division IA Indiana State University in Terre Haute, Indiana called me knowing we had an open date on our schedule. They had just hired a new coach and wanted a home game as an opportunity to basically beat up on someone and prove the new coach was on the right track. This wasn't just a game—it was a paycheck. We had a chance to play another team, but with a cash guarantee. I was Athletic Director at the time and I knew we needed the money. I also knew Sister Elise wanted us to make that much-needed money, but she was concerned our boys were going to get hurt. Indiana State had had three times as many scholarships as we did, and that meant they had their pick of players to recruit,

We had a lot of new guys starting, but we also had nineteen seniors on our team who had been through three seasons without losing a regular season football game.

When I announced the game during the winter football banquet a lot of people were nervous. This was a Division One team—it wasn't going to be an easy game. The coaching team - asked the players if they were up to the task. They said they were and spent the winter in the weight room physically and mentally preparing.

Nine days before our scheduled game I went to Terre Haute to watch Eastern Illinois play Indiana State. When their players came on the field the eye test said Saint Francis was in big trouble. The Indiana State players were bigger, faster, and stronger athletes. They ended up losing to Eastern Illinois, a team that had been in the Division One IAA playoffs the previous year. On the ride home the coaches and I worried that we might have bitten off more than we could chew, but we were committed so we decided to go for it and hope for the best. Still I did a lot of praying in those nine days before the game.

Saint Francis went to Indiana State and played their opening game in 2005 on a hot September afternoon. They went with the attitude of expecting to win, which I think is a big part of what fueled our guys against some pretty impossible odds. We went after them and humiliated them. We won the game 42-10 took our check and went home. We proved ourselves and earned the respect of a lot of big schools. Purdue replaced us on Indiana State's schedule in 2006.

The Cougars went on to record their fourth straight undefeated regular season and another league championship. Along the way our only test that year was against McKendree 28-21 at their home opener. In the post season our Cougars rolled past Pikeville (Kentucky), Georgetown, and Morningside before having to face Carroll College once more in the National Championship.

This was our second straight appearance in a title game. On December 17, 2005, we stood there in Jim Carroll Stadium in Savannah, Tennessee all knotted up with anticipation and nerves. When the day was over Carroll College won its fourth consecutive title 27-10. The Saint Francis guys had worked hard, sacrificed, and put forth a gallant effort, but had come up short once more.

We could have been depressed, could have focused only on the failure. But I reminded the team on the ride home that "defeat" is adversity and adversity is part of life. You can either let it beat you down or propel you forward.

The 2006 Season

In the fall of 2006 we started out fast and hard rolling over early opponents before winning a stiff fight with conference rival Ohio Dominican, 21-17. We were tested further in a 21-20 win against Geneva en route to completing our fifth consecutive undefeated regular season and winning another

conference championship. In the playoffs we had another bat-
tle against Bethel, but we won 42-35 in the quarterfinals.
We beat Saint Xavier the next week in the semi-finals before
making our third consecutive trip to the finals at Jim Carroll
Stadium, this time against the University of Sioux Falls (South
Dakota).

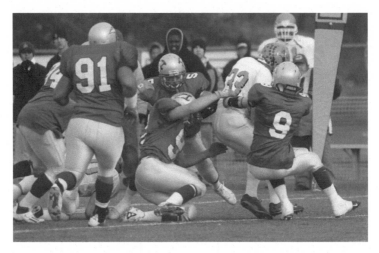

Cougar defense gangs up to make a tackle and stop a run.

That game day was unusually warm—a sunny 72 degrees
Fahrenheit at game time. Sioux Falls won the toss and elected
to kick off. We started off strong—putting together a good
drive capped by a gutsy call on a fourth down just outside field
goal range that set up the first score and gave us a 7-0 lead. But

that lead soon narrowed when Sioux Falls used a 37-yard TD pass to put points on the board.

From that point, the game seesawed back and forth. Saint Francis took a 13-6 lead but that was soon answered y by an 89-yard return on the following kick-off. Sioux Falls took the lead at the start of the third quarter on a short field goal after being stopped at the Saint Francis six-yard line.

On our next possession an errant snap sent the ball over punter Clint Bontempo's head and ended up giving Sioux Falls the ball at our fifteen-yard line. Two plays later the score was Sioux Falls 23, Saint Francis 13. We gave it all we got in that last quarter, but ended up losing 23-19. We had lost our third consecutive national championship game.

From the outside it seems like it should be easy to win at that level—after all we won all the games going up to the national championship. We had a strong, experienced and talented team. But it's not just about that. To get to the national level you have to be better than good, but you also have to score a few breaks. A ball flying too high or bouncing one time too many can change everything. We got there in 2004, 2005, and 2006, but just getting to the national level wasn't enough.

The locker room was silent after that loss. So many of our guys had been on the team for multiple seasons, and they really thought this would be the year. They were disappointed and depressed. I stepped into the center of the circle of my team and gave them a long look. They were sweaty and dirty and dejected as hell. "I am so proud of you," I said to them. "We are a great team, and on this day, it took another great team to beat us. They deserve our respect. Let's honor our opponent." And the guys did. At Saint Francis character matters—more than winning, and this was a moment to remind these young people about what was most important. Not what happens on the field, but what happens after you put away your cleats and take off the uniform.

Chapter 11

Plateau Years

The 2007 Season

Saint Francis came back to prepare for our 2007 season optimistic, despite losing our third consecutive national championship contest the fall before. The handout the school used for recruiting proudly proclaimed a "Decade of Dominance" for its
10th anniversary edition. Saint Francis and our team had reason
to be proud and optimistic. The Cougars were coming off our
5th consecutive undefeated regular season. We had appeared
in three consecutive NAIA National Championships. We had
won eight straight MFSA Mideast League titles, five straight
outright championships, and 51 consecutive regular-season

games, including 36 straight home games. I had a 91-20 overall record at Saint Francis, including 62-5 over the last five
seasons. The Cougars had the best win and loss record of any
team in Indiana, a state that includes that other little Catholic
college, Notre Dame.

We had far surpassed the expectations set in those initial
meetings back when we had no equipment, no locker rooms,
and no field. This had gone from a dream to an outstanding
reality.

We had lost some key players to graduation, but we had a
crop of forty-five talented freshmen many of who were named
to their respective all-conference teams as high school seniors.

With all that accomplishment, however, come high expectations. The school and the city fully expected us to return to
Savannah, Tennessee for our fourth shot at winning a national
championship. We began the season ranked high in the polls.
Street & Smith ranked us number one while in the NAIA
Spring Football Top 10 rankings Saint Francis was listed at
number two, right behind the University of Sioux Falls.

The Cougars opened our season at home against William
Penn and galloped to a 71-7 victory. The next week we followed

up with a 55-3 shellacking of Pikeville (KY) in the first of three games on the road. The team struggled a bit against Saint. Ambrose the next week, but managed to post a 20-7 victory that set up a showdown with conference rival Ohio Dominican in Columbus, Ohio. Ohio Dominican had been waiting for this game ever since losing 21-17 to us the previous season.

ODU scored first but the Cougars answered that touchdown with Marcus Rush carrying the ball in from two yards out. With Rhys Barnhart's kick, the score was tied. ODU scored on three possessions in the second quarter to lead 23-7 after a 31-yard field goal with 3:46 remaining in the half. Danny Carter's seven-yard scamper closed that gap with just 34 ticks left in the half. Jeff Weddings pass for two failed leaving the halftime score ODU 23, USF 13.

Another touchdown in the third quarter narrowed the score to 23-20 until ODU added a final TD with 2:42 remaining in the game. In the end, we couldn't pull off another touchdown and we lost.

It was the Cougars first regular season loss since 2001 when we lost to Tri-State. The critics were quick to jump on us as if they'd been waiting for us to stumble.

But it was the team I cared about. I drew them together in a huddle at the end of the field and threw down a challenge. "What are you going to do now?" I asked them. "Are you going to let this loss undo all your hard work or are you going to learn from it and move on?"

The answer came the next week with a 57-7 thumping of Marian followed by one-sided victories over Taylor, Walsh, and Urbana. On November 3, 2007 the Cougars faced the number eighteen-ranked Malone in Canton, Ohio. The first half of that game was close with Saint Francis leading 10-7 at the break. In the third quarter two more touchdowns increased our lead to 24-7. Malone added a field goal early in the fourth to cut the score to USF 24-10 but then our Danny Carter scored and brought us to 31-10. The game finished 31-17 a victory that cemented the team's confidence again. Saint Francis finished the regular season 9-1 with a 42-13 whipping of rival #6 Saint Xavier.

We were back in the playoffs with our first match against Lindenwood (MO). During the pregame while the teams were on the field warming up one of the Lindenwood players struck up a conversation with a USF co-ed who was helping out with pre-game details. "What is it about this place no one can win here?" the player asked. "Is it the field, the fans? What makes it so hard for teams to win here?"

The co-ed looked at the Lindenwood player and smiled. "I don't know, but you're about to find out."

Every time I hear that story, it makes me smile. It speaks to how the outside world viewed us—a team that no one thought could come together yet surpassed everyone's expectations, including mine.

Lindenwood received the opening kickoff and promptly marched down the field and put seven points on the board in the first two minutes of play. We tried to come back against that, but ended up being forced to give up the ball on downs.

The Lions took the ball and put another seven points on the scoreboard to lead 14-0. On our next opportunity we again failed to score and Lindenwood moved the ball inside our 25, but failed to get a first down on a crucial 4th down and 1 situation.

At that point the game changed and the Cougars brought out their offensive game scoring 35 unanswered points while holding Lindenwood scoreless. We weren't going to lose at home and we sure weren't going to lose to a team with the same name as the large cemetery across the railroad tracks from D'Arcy Stadium.

The team did what they had been taught to do. They took the adversity they'd been handed and turned it around. It was a game I'll never forget not just because of how the Cougars flipped the score but because my son Pat was at my side for the whole game. Pat was only twenty-seven at the time, only a year older than I was when I got my first head coach job. Pat had a thorough knowledge of the game and understood how I thought and how I liked to run my team so we operated as a unit. It's probably one of my proudest moments—watching my son carry the coaching ball forward.

The NAIA Quarter Final against #4 Bethel (TN) the following week was one of those games that will be long remembered. When Saint Francis relinquished the ball to Bethel with 8:30 left in the 4th quarter (and the Cougars leading 27-14), it looked as if all the Cougars needed to do was coast home to victory, but the momentum changed almost in a heartbeat. Bethel ran the ball and scored, with just four minutes left. We tried to get the ball back down to our goalposts, but the drive stalled when running back Daniel Carter was brought down at the Bethel nineteen-yard line after snagging Wedding's pass short of a first down on a fourth and 10 situation.

Bethel moved the ball quickly and capped off a successful drive with a 30-yard run to tie the score with less than two minutes remaining. The point-after kick was blocked, which gave our Cougars new life and hope. After the kick-off Wedding moved the Cougars quickly to the Bethel thirty-two, but a holding call moved the ball back to the forty-two. After another play, the Cougars were again penalized for holding and found themselves on their own forty-eight with twenty-six seconds remaining.

What happened next is the kind of stuff you only see in movies or read in fiction. If I hadn't been there myself I wouldn't have believed it. I've seen some incredible last-minute plays but this one topped them all. Wedding moved our ball to the Bethel thirty-five-yard line. With 5.9 seconds and one timeout left we gambled on running one more play before attempting a field goal. The play moved the ball forward but time expired before the timeout was called.

That could have been it. Done, and over, and another loss. However, Bethel was whistled for a facemask infraction, which gave us an extra play since the game cannot end on a penalty call. The ball was spotted at the Bethel twenty-six. Rhys Barnhart stepped up after two consecutive Bethel timeouts to ice him and kicked the ball perfectly between the uprights giving our team an unbelievable 30-27 victory and a trip to the NAIA semi-final game against Carroll College in Helena, Montana.

I hadn't had to call on Barnhart to kick a field goal the whole season. But he was cool, focused, had a good leg, and was an effective and deadly accurate kicker. When we needed it most, he stepped up and performed.

Saint Francis quarterback Jeff Wedding was presented with the MVP award for leading his team to victory. But then Wedding took the award and immediately passed it to Barnhart. That was the kind of guy and leader Wedding was and the kind of team we had. They knew it was a total team effort not the work of one superstar.

The dramatic win over Bethel only fueled Cougar fever and raised expectations for their return to the finals. We'd come so close so many times and everyone thought *this* would be our year.

To get there we had one more opponent to beat—and it was a familiar one: #2 ranked Carroll College of Helena, Montana. Saint Francis had lost three previous encounters to the Saints. We lost the semi-final matchup in 2003, and the championship game in both 2004 and 2005.

On the flight to Montana for our semi-final match the team seemed excited and upbeat. For many of them being on a plane was a new experience and the whole thing seemed like an adventure. But by the time we were at breakfast on Saturday morning the mood had changed markedly. Reality was setting in, and the team was quiet, keeping to themselves. One of my other coaches remarked that it was so quiet you could hear the silver hitting the porcelain plates in the hotel restaurant.

I understood that need for quiet. After the meal I walked around the hotel not talking to anyone just thinking and planning for the game ahead. Being alone, even if there are dozens of people around me, gives me time to focus and center myself. The pressure of coaching is enormous regardless of what level you are at and just like my players I need to take time to get into the mental game long before the coin toss.

Carroll had a state-of-the art stadium with four thousand permanent seats and luxury boxes above them. Behind the seats and inside the building there were heaters to warm you as you waited on your food order from vendors like Pizza Hut and other well-know fast food companies.

Game day dawned at a balmy 6 degrees Fahrenheit. The pre-game tradition was to come out on the field in shorts and sleeveless T-shirts to 'test' the field. I wasn't about to let them play like that so I made sure every player had thermal under-wear, hand warmers, and foot warmers so they'd stay warm for the hours we'd be playing.

There's a good reason people call this field and place 'the tundra.' The field is grass, not field turf, and on game day, it was hard as concrete and frozen. Just days earlier they'd removed snow from the field. Carroll, being native to the area and well acquainted with these field conditions had their players wear shoes with spikes, which gave them better footing and easier maneuvering on the icy ground. Our players were in regular football shoes, which reduced our traction and hindered our ability to make sharp turns. Little things like that can make all the difference as we soon found out.

Saint Francis scored early in the first quarter when Wedding lofted a pass to Bo Thompson as he sped down the sidelines. The pass was perfect and Thompson scurried into the end zone giving the Cougars the lead and its only score on a play that covered 72 yards.

On each of the next several possessions, it seemed we couldn't move the ball. Carroll was able to move into the red zone, but on each occasion our stubborn defense held and they had to settle for a field goal. They added the last just before halftime and led 9-7.

In the third quarter Carroll forced Saint Francis three and out and scored, late in the third to take a 16-7 lead. In the fourth quarter, their receiver sprinted forty yards to bring the score to 23-7.

Getting the ball back we finally got some traction and moved down the field well into Saints territory. The drive stalled on two successive failed passed that were interfered with but no foul called. The second time our receiver lost his temper that resulted in a major penalty being assessed against

Saint Francis. The young man was ranting irate at the call but instead of reaming him out I held on to him and talked him down.

When it was over we had lost another chance to advance to the championship game. Players were disappointed and heartbroken afterwards standing in the frigid cold. Several of these players were seniors who had a dream and they mourned for the loss of that dream on that cold day, far away from home in a strange place.

The 2008 Season

In 2008, new NAIA rules were instituted that shortened the play clock to speed up play or maybe to shorten games for TV viewers. It would also increase slots for advertising revenue. The NCAA had been the first to make this change, and the NAIA followed suit although NAIA games are not generally televised.

For us this meant new strategies. We normally averaged eighty plays a game but now I wasn't sure we'd have time to fit in sixty.

We went into the pre-season with high expectations both from the school and the players. We might have lost to Carroll and missed a national title again, but we were still a strong team that was used to winning.

Coach Donley watching the action

2008 was just as good a year. We plowed through our regular season winning by an average of 49-12. The Cougars jumped on number 10 Saint Ambrose, scoring early and building a 29-0 lead before coasting to a 43-14 victory. We followed that with a nearly perfect game against Ohio Dominican that ended at 35-0, a nice comeback after our last game against them.

We beat Marian, Walsh, and Malone before finishing the regular season undefeated with a 47-30 slashing of number 18 Saint Xavier. This was our sixth undefeated regular season in seven years, and our ninth conference championship. In that time period, we had won fifty-three straight home games and had won eighty-five games against eight losses overall.

Part of this success was due to the Carter brothers. Paul was a defensive back with the potential to play professionally. Daniel possessed speed combined with maneuverability and a sixth sense to ferret out the smallest hole in the other team's defense allowing him to run the ball in situations others might avoid. The two brothers were also intensely loyal and protective of one another. In the third quarter of our game against Saint Xavier Paul ended up on the ground after a play. Daniel sprinted across the field to his brother's side that earned the team an infraction for having an unauthorized player on the field. But that was Daniel—loyal to a fault. Later in the game, Daniel made up for his transgression. He took a pitch out from quarterback Tierney, scampered around the left side and broke free for a thirty-yard gain, the last ten or so yards of which he completed running *backwards* after being spun around by a Saint Xavier defender. Even running backwards, Daniel was faster than most.

In the playoffs we faced number 11 Union (KY) in the first round and won 58-3. That was followed with a more difficult 31-20 victory over number 8 Cumberlands in the quarterfinals to set up a second showdown with Sioux Falls.

We went to Sioux City, South Dakota, to face the same team we had lost to in 2006. Sioux Falls was ranked number one and on a mission to win another national championship. The sky was sunny, but the temperature was barely got over zero, and there was a stiff 40-mph wind blowing straight down the north-south orientation of the field. It seemed like the state was trying to convince us to go home.

It was to be a long cold afternoon for our Cougars. Sioux Falls scored twice in the first period to go up 10-0 and built on that in the second, adding two more scores to lead 24-0 at the half. Our defense held Sioux Falls scoreless in the second half, which put us in position to score early in the third and turn the game momentum. Then we fumbled away the ball on the one-yard line. Our only score came early in the fourth period on a twenty-six-yard pass from Mickey Cassidy to Jared Clodfelter. It was too little, too late, and we ended with Sioux Falls 24 and Saint Francis 6.

For the fifth straight year we lost to the team that would eventually become the national champion. It was a disappointing end to what had been a perfect season filled with many positives.

The 2009 Season

After all those years of success, we hit a bump in the road in 2009. It was a season plagued with unseen off-the-field issues with administration and budget cuts.

That fall began in a positive direction. The Cougars still had lots of talent and experience, including running back Daniel Carter and quarterback Shaine Tierney who gave our team a multidimensional game both in running and in passing. We won our first four games handily, and then faced tighter competition against Walsh. Carter scored on a forty-two-yard run with 6:48 left in the third quarter to put the Cougars up

20-7. Walsh, however, wasn't ready to concede and scored to cut the lead to 20-14 with 1:19 left in the third. They tried to score again in the fourth quarter, but we held onto the ball and prevailed 20-14.

For game seven we stepped out of the NAIA to take on NCAA Division II team Missouri Science & Technology in Rolla, Missouri. At that point we thought we were going to repeat our previous years' success. We were 6-0 and had disposed of nine straight NCAA opponents of all levels over the past ten years. But on that rainy, muddy day in Missouri the Miners beat us, 39-37.

The next week we bounced back by chewing up Olivet Nazarene 56-7. It appeared whatever had gone wrong in Missouri was fixed and the team was back in their groove.

Late in the game with Olivet the Tigers were deep in their own territory on the far side of the field at about the 20-yard line when play was stopped because an Olivet player went down. During the official timeout running back Daniel Carter who had a habit of making quips shouted in the direction of Saint Francis President Sister Elis, "You better pray for them, Sister. It's the only way they are going to get out of here!"

Carter didn't know it then, but a week later he'd be the one asking for prayers.

We were back on our home field the next weekend facing Saint Xavier to determine the conference champion. We went in with confidence. We'd dominated Saint Xavier many times before and they had never been able to contain Daniel Carter.

It looked for a moment like this might be another one of those easy wins. Carter broke loose and charged down the sidelines, with no one from Saint Xavier even close to catching him. Suddenly inside the twenty Carter drew up and limped to the sidelines. He had pulled a hamstring. He was finished for the day.

Ironically Carter pulled up lame at nearly the same spot the Olivet player had gone down the week before when Carter made his quip to Sister Elis. Without Carter we had lost our primary offensive weapon. The rest of the team poured it on and the game went back and forth the score close, but when the horn sounded Saint Xavier had won 36-24 and ended Saint Francis's fifty-nine-game home win streak.

Wounded, but not out of the finals yet Saint Francis only had to beat conference rival and fellow Indiana school Taylor to secure a place in the NAIA playoffs for the eleventh straight year. Carter's status was questionable and starting quarterback Shaine Tierney was also dealing with an injury. Both tried to come off the bench and contribute but it wasn't enough. Our offense never quite clicked into gear and we lost to the Trojans for the first time in a decade. Saint Francis was a much better team than the Trojans but not on that day.

I was stunned. My Cougars had lost for the third time in four games. That kind of streak hadn't happened since the school's first football season twelve years earlier when the team finished 2-8. In 2009 the Cougars finished 7-3 and the unexpected loss to Taylor also prevented Saint Francis from participating in the NAIA playoffs for the first time since that same inaugural season in 1998.

Before I allowed myself to think about the loss and what it meant I focused on talking to my players. I saw Danny Carter sitting on a windowsill outside the locker room devastated about his injury and letting down his team. I sat down beside him and drew him into a hug and reminded him that he had done his best and that was all anyone—including him—could expect. Being a good man, a good person, was what mattered most. The rest was just a game. It was something I told my guys often—this moment in time wasn't the most important one. Let the disappointment go and focus on the future, on the next play, the next life choice.

I felt like I had failed. Failed my school. Failed my players. I thought about what had gone wrong for a long time and realized my difficult year with the administration and other stresses had boiled over into my coaching. All those lessons I had given my players about handling adversity had flown out the window in my own head. I'd learned a hard lesson, one that was hopefully going to stick with me into the next season.

The 2010 Season

At halftime during our first game of 2010 I sat the team down in the locker room and talked to them about stepping up. I had a lot of inexperienced freshman and underclassmen on the team, and I wanted them to take the game seriously, to grow up, and find their place as men on the field.

The speech worked its magic. We went back onto the field facing Saint Ambrose and behind 17-0. We were inside the Bees own five-yard line when our defensive ends Rex Drabenstot and Anthony Moore caught the Bees quarterback Danny Tharp in the end zone for a safety and made the score 17-2. A later forty-five yard Tierney pass to Jared Clodfelter, followed by an extra point kick brought us to 17-9.

In the fourth quarter, Saint Ambrose was ahead 20-9, but Tierney made a sixty-nine-yard pass to Austin Coleman. That touchdown coupled with a two-point conversion by Bo Frey cut the deficit to 20-17.

That infused the team with confidence. We scored again then forced another three and out to grab the ball and finish scoring with one final touchdown and PAT ending the game at 31-20.

There was to be no rest, we traveled to Indianapolis the next week to face archrival number thirteen Marian. After building a 28-10 lead at the half our offense lost its steam and watched the Knights creep up to twenty-five points. With only four minutes left Marian was sensing victory.

Then quarterback Shaine Tierney started to pass, didn't find anyone open, but managed to slip through a seam in the defense wide enough to scramble thirteen yards for a first down effectively ending the Knights' thoughts of a come-from-behind victory.

When we faced conference rival Malone the next week we once again found ourselves on the tail end of the score, 17-10 entering the fourth quarter. We managed to tie the score with a one-yard run with 8:23 left in the quarter. Then Aaron Knight returned a punt seventy-one yards to set up the score on an eleven-yard pass from Tierney to Clodfelter, giving us a 23-17 lead. The extra point was missed giving the ball back to Malone with 6:34 remaining.

Malone wasn't known for its passing but the team managed to move the ball to a first and goal at the Saint Francis eight-yard line with 1:06 on the clock. Malone, out of timeouts, spiked a third down pass with 22.8 seconds left to set up their final play. But the pass was a little too high, probably because Saint Francis defensive end Tony Moore had hold of the quarterback's ankles. It was another climatic finish for the Cougars.

Number eight Walsh was the next opponent blocking our path. After the last three weeks no one was expecting anything but drama, and that's what we got, with a tie score of 7-7 at halftime. At the end of the third quarter, Walsh connected on a forty-two-yard play that put the Cavaliers up 14-7, but at the last second, our quarterback Tierney connected with Armondo Bustamante on a sixteen-yard play to knot the score at 14-14. In the last quarter, Tierney pushed his way into the end zone on a one-yard keeper to give Saint Francis the win. That game was my 250th career win.

Saint Francis had little trouble rolling over our next three foes—Trinity International, Missouri Science and Technology, and Olivet Nazarene—by a 46-9 average. Then we went up against rival and number three Saint Xavier in Chicago. The game was ours to lose, and we did exactly that. Saint Xavier made the plays that counted and walked away with a 30-6 victory and the MSFA Mideast Conference title for the second consecutive year.

We closed out the regular season with a difficult 33-21 win over Taylor before entering the playoffs. We headed to St. Charles, Missouri to face number five Lindenwood (and the nation's top-ranked scoring offense, averaging 53.9 points a game). The two teams traded touchdowns and the lead until we recovered a Lindenwood fumble at our own forty-five-yard-line with 3:47 left. We finished that game with a win at 46-38.

We returned to Chicago the following week to face Saint Xavier for the second time in three weeks in a quarter final matchup, but the Cougars from the Southside of Chicago were ready for us and ended our season with a 40-21 victory.

What I'll remember most about that 2010 team, though, wasn't the games or the plays on the field. It was the way my guys supported each other. We had a receiver who ran a very fast forty and was a valuable asset to the Saint Francis Football team. He went home in the summer of 2010 for break, but then failed to appear at football camp or return any of my multiple phone calls. He was a poor kid from a large city and a tough environment, and I worried he had dropped out or transferred.

A bit later he showed up in my office, begging for a second chance. He had his head down, and he was mumbling. I told him to raise his head and speak clearly. When I heard his story, I brought him to the team's senior council, which was made up of all eleven senior players. I asked them if they would allow this young man to come before them and tell his story, and then vote on his return. The council was mad. They felt like he had abandoned the team and didn't deserve to be heard.

But there was one senior who said he wanted to hear what his former teammate had to say. He said their fellow Cougar deserved that opportunity.

Everyone assumed the young man had left for selfish reasons, but I knew this kid and knew his history. He stood before the senior council and told them that when he went home he'd hoped he could be a positive influence on his younger brother who was involved in a gang. His younger brother had been in fights and even been shot. But his efforts and he was finally convinced to return to Saint Francis and make something of his own life. My team made me proud that day. The player who had initially vetoed this player's return became his biggest supporter. Two other teammates came to his aid and allowed him to live in their house for free the entire school year.

It wasn't that 250th game or any of the wins we had chalked up in the previous years that told me I was doing a good job as a coach. It was that moment when one of my players needed help and the others stood around him and offered their shoulders for support that left me humbled and moved. And grateful to God for giving me a job that helped foster the growth of such incredible young men.

The 2011 Season

Expectations were high and the mood confident heading into our thirteenth season. We opened the season against pesky Saint Ambrose at an away game in Davenport, Iowa. Saint Ambrose scored first to lead 7-0, but we answered with two touchdowns, bringing us to 14-7. At the half Saint Ambrose was back on top, 21-14. In the third The Bees added another touchdown, but missed the extra point and led 27-14 before we put two more touchdowns on the board to regain the lead at 28-27. With 9:28 left in the fourth quarter after another Saint Ambrose touchdown, we ran a twelve-play seventy-yard drive directed by quarterback Justin Bowser that culminated with redshirt freshman Anton Campbell's second touchdown. We held onto that lead and prevailed 34-33 in yet another come-from-behind victory.

That victory helped elevate Saint Francis to the number two ranking in the following week. We went on to beat McKendree 33-7 and newcomer Concordia 69-0.

Then we were back playing Saint Xavier. The two teams had been rated number one and number two in the recent

NAIA poll. There was plenty of hype and high expectations on and off the field, but the result was the same as the last three meetings.

We took advantage of Saint Xavier mistakes to grab an early 10-0 lead, but the game went downhill from there. Saint Francis led for the last time 24-23 in the third after Austin Coleman's ninety-eight-yard kickoff return. The 42-31 loss was Saint Francis's fourth consecutive loss to these other Cougars from Chicago. We struggled in our next game against Walsh a week later, and it took us two overtimes to finally win that game 42-41.

We went home to play Marian, who was ready for us this time. On our own field they crushed us 40-13. It was our first loss to the Knights and our second straight home loss.

The team rebounded after that racking up four straight wins averaging almost 47 points a game and giving up a mere 13. We finished our regular season 8-2 and faced number seven Missouri Valley in Marshall, Missouri. Saint Francis broke a 14-14 tie with two scores in the fourth quarter to win 28-14.

That victory gave us the opportunity to travel to Georgetown, Kentucky for a date with number three Georgetown in the quarterfinals. We made a gallant effort, but it wasn't enough to overcome Georgetown's strength and we lost 28-14. The Cougars finished the 2011 season 9-3.

The 2012 Season

We opened the 2012 season with a 46-10 victory over Texas College and a 39-31 win over NCAA Division III Wisconsin Stevens Point. Next up was always troublesome Saint Ambrose.

That game taught me not to take anything for granted, especially victory. Saint Ambrose clung to a slim 7-6 lead until Saint Francis quarterback Wes Hunsucker connected with Austin Coleman on a seventy-yard play with 7:47 left in the fourth quarter. Anton Campbell barreled into the end zone to give the Cougars a 14-7 lead.

It all fell apart for us after that. We had a blocked thirty-four-yard field goal attempt. Then we missed an opportunity when we had the ball on our own twenty-three-yard line with 3:22 remaining. Saint Ambrose took the ball back, made a fifty-yard pass and then a touchdown followed by a two-point conversion, which gave them the lead and the win, 15-14.

We had a moment of victory against Concordia (76-14) before meeting number one Saint Xavier in Chicago and leaving with a hard-earned 25-13 victory. Then we lost to Marian again 45-38.

That uneven season continued with four wins against William Penn (28-19), Sienna Heights (31-7), Taylor (21-0), and Lindenwood Belleville (44-7) before we faced number eleven Baker University in the NAIA playoffs and winning 22-17.

We were up against Marian for the second time in the quarterfinals in Indianapolis. Saint Francis scored first but Marian scored four times to take a 24-7 lead in the third quarter before we cut that lead to 24-14. In the end, Marian beat us 45-34.

We finished the season 9-3, but won a share of the MSFA Mideast Conference title. Again it was not our best year. Good players rotate out replaced by new ones that are coming in and need time to build their skills. Opponents that had played us so many times were undoubtedly working strategies to combat the wins we had had in previous years. Everyone was learning and growing--and that meant that not every game was going to be an easy win. Still I felt our effort and commitment hadn't been where we wanted it.

The 2013 Season

Of the twelve opponents we faced during the 2013 season nine were rated and one, Robert Morris (IL), while not rated was well regarded. It meant our team had to always be at its best. We had been really working hard to develop new talent. Some of our best players were upperclassmen now and it was making a difference.

In the season opener we traveled to Oskaloosa, Iowa to face number sixteen William Penn. The game was still close at the end of three quarters with number five Saint Francis holding a slim 17-13 lead. In the fourth quarter, our boys scored twice in a little over a four-minute span to put the game out of reach at 31-13.

The next week we came back to home turf to face Saint Ambrose with the memory of the Bees' come-from-behind last minute win the year before still fresh in our minds. The game seesawed back and forth until Seth Coate's reception of an eight-yard pass from Josh Miller in the back of the end zone giving us a 38-28 lead with 11:49 remaining on the clock. Then things started getting interesting.

Saint Ambrose added a field goal with 8:31 left and added another touchdown at 3:37, cutting the lead to 38-37. The attempted pass for two on the extra point failed but the Bees were not finished. After getting the ball back they drove into field goal position, but their forty-one-yard attempt went wide. The clock ran out and we chalked up another victory.

The following week we went to Des Moines, Iowa to face number seven Grand View. We were upbeat going into the game coming off wins against two very good teams. Then quarterback Josh Miller aggravated an ankle injury and Anton Campbell suffered a knee injury. That killed our offensive punch early in the first quarter and we lost 23-7.

Our next game against number 25 Siena Heights in Adrian, Michigan looked bad with our hosts going into the locker room leading 17-14 at the half.

I pulled the team together and reminded them of all the hard work they had put in of how they had overcome worse and how they had everything they needed inside themselves.

When we returned to the field the fans that had traveled to the away game cheered enthusiastically. The boys got it together and we put a couple touchdowns on the board capped by Seth Coates' twenty-eight-yard pass reception from back-up quarterback David Yoder. We finished that game with a 28-17 win.

We had a slow start in our next game against number ten Saint Xavier. We were behind 7-3 late in the first half when backup quarterback David Yoder scored on a one-yard plunge with little over a minute remaining to give us the lead for good, 10-7. Then came back on the field to add twenty-one points in the third quarter and fourteen more in the fourth to cruise to a 45-20 win. We followed that with a 37-20 win over number twenty Saint Francis of Illinois.

Things were looking up for 2013 but on the bus ride home from Illinois the team bus carrying the defense was involved in a horrific accident when a car went out of control and smashed into the bus. The accident took the life of one young man and left a young woman in very critical condition.

The crash resulted in our team busses getting separated forcing part of us to wait at a toll road plaza while another bus could be dispatched to the scene to pick up the rest. The accident left a deep impact on our players that showed up the following week.

The next week we faced an unranked but dangerously strong Robert Morris (IL) team at home and found ourselves down 14-0 late in the first half. It took a while for us to get our mojo back, but we finally managed to score two quick touchdowns in the final 1:11 of first half to tie the score. We added another ten points in the third to lead 24-14 and it looked as though the day was going to turn out okay. Robert Morris scored with 10:39 on the clock to make it close and we traded the ball back and forth until Robert Morris scored the game-winning touchdown on a six-yard pass with just 33 seconds left on the clock.

We followed that game with a 54-0 win over Concordia and a 20-12 victory over Taylor before facing number twenty-seven Marian at home for the league title. Marian jumped to an early lead and led 17-7 at the half, but the Cougars bared their claws in the second half outscoring the Knights 34-7 to win 41-24. Saint Francis finished the regular season 8-2 and MSFA Mideast Conference Champions.

That year, the Cougars entered the NAIA playoffs in a hopeful mood. The game pitted number six Saint Francis against number nine Faulkner University from Montgomery, Alabama. Faulkner was loaded with transfers and athleticism. They had forty-eight transfers on their roster and seemed like a formidable team.

During pregame warm ups several Faulkner players started talking trash and trying to taunt fans in the James Shields Pavilion at the south end of D'Arcy Stadium. The weather was cold in the lower twenties with thirty mile per hour wind gusts out of the north.

By the half we were leading 20-7. Then the snow came in the third quarter, turning the playing surface white, hiding the lines, and making movement more difficult. Neither team scored in the third, but Faulkner added a touchdown early in the fourth to trail 20-13 after missing the extra point.

Then the game got really interesting. After getting the ball with 7:26 left on the clock at their own nineteen-yard line Faulkner moved to a first and goal at the Saint Francis ten. Three plays later we were called for interference with a receiver in the end zone. The ball was now on the two-yard line with 1:39 remaining. The Faulkner Eagles had four shots to get the ball over the goal line but failed. We took possession in the driving snow in blizzard conditions and David Yoder completed a gutsy pass on the third down that allowed Saint Francis to keep the ball and run out the clock preserving our win.

The next week we traveled to Williamsburg, Kentucky to take on number one Cumberlands in a quarterfinal matchup. Cumberlands took the lead scoring first late in the first quarter and leading 21-7 at the half. They added another touchdown in the third to lead 28-7 before our guys could get back on the scoreboard early in the fourth to trim the lead to 28-14. Still we lost that game.

We finished 2013 the same as the year before—9-3 and this time winners of the MSFA Mideast conference title.

The following week, I was named Mid-States Football Association Mideast League Coach of the Year for the ninth time in sixteen seasons. It was my seventeenth coach of the year honor in thirty-five football seasons. I was grateful to God, so very grateful, for this opportunity with Saint Francis and to be blessed with such great players and support, but a part of me still longed for that national title. All those years were building blocks driving the Cougars closer to that goal. But like any good football game the gains are often offset by losses and victory is never a sure thing.

Chapter 12

Stumbling, the Key Stepping Stone to Success

Coach Kevin Donley was inducted into the NAIA Hall of Fame at the NAIA Hall of Fame Banquet at the American Football Coaches Association Convention in Indianapolis, IN on January 12, 2014. Here he celebrates the 2016 Championship with the team in Daytona after being interviewed by ESPN.

The 2014 Season

Saint Francis had experienced fifteen straight very successful years. Winning had become expected. And with that kind of cocky assuredness comes a little laziness. The team was starting to take what we had accomplished for granted. All along I had prepared them for adversity, but this time the challenge was within them.

The team commitment began to wane. The first subtle signs of this showed in the less-than-enthusiastic participation during the winter in the weight room.

In the season opener against first-year Missouri Baptist the Cougars fumbled the ball away in the first two possessions and didn't score until 3:06 of the first quarter. From there, we built a 35-3 lead at the half. I brought in the backups in the third quarter and we ended that game 42-10. It was a sizeable victory but I could feel that something was off.

The next Saturday against William Penn made that knot of tension in my gut get bigger. The Statesmen were unrated and although respected not generally considered a threat. During the pregame warm-ups it was evident William Penn showed up emotionally and physically ready to play. The Statesmen were a team that liked to run and their offensive line made huge holes in our defense. That running helped them to a 13-6 lead after the first quarter. By the half we led 20-13 but William Penn tied that at the end of the third quarter. We were up 27-20 in the fourth and thought we had it nailed until the Statesmen scored to come within one point with 1:38 on the clock, and then secured their comeback win with a two-point conversion.

The next weekend we bounced back with a 27-13 win over number 25 Saint Ambrose in Davenport, Iowa and came home to get ready to meet number eight Grand View. I was a little nervous about our chances. Grand View had won the national championship the previous fall and two of my guys, Campbell and Miller, were still battling injuries.

Saint Francis trailed 7-3 after the first period and led 9-7 at the half on the strength of two Nix field goals. Grand View went ahead on a score in the third to lead 14-9. They added their final points on a forty-four-yard run with 2:08 on the clock. We tried but our offense simply wasn't there.

The next week we lost an unprecedented third straight game at home to Siena Heights 27-21. That was followed by a humiliating 53-16 defeat at Saint Xavier.

The Cougars were 2-4 and 0-1 in conference. All of a sudden we were in a place we hadn't been in since the first year of the program in 1998. Trust me we had a lot of locker room lectures about getting in the game zone again. I reminded the guys that wins are never guaranteed and if they didn't get their act together all those years of hard work would be for nothing.

The team rebounded the following week with a 42-20 win over number 18 ranked Saint Francis (IL) and followed that with a 38-20 victory over number twelve Robert Morris (IL). We returned home to whip Concordia 30-14 and Taylor 42-0. We had recovered just enough to be in position of sneaking into the playoffs—but only if we could win against number nine Marian.

At the beginning, it looked like we might achieve the improbable. We built an 18-3 lead, but Marian scored just seconds before halftime to trim the lead to 18-10. We held onto our lead until midway through the third quarter. Marian grabbed two touchdowns then added 17 points in the fourth to run away with a 51-18 win.

The loss put an end to a frustrating and embarrassing season. Saint Francis still finished a respectable 6-5, 4-2 in MSFA MEL, but I was not happy. I knew my guys had been phoning it in, riding a wave of confidence from the years before when we were able to pull off a last-minute win.

But the problem wasn't entirely in the locker room. My team needed an attitude makeover and that was about to start at the top.

The 2015 Season

The disappointment of the 2014 season hit the team and me with a bucket of cold icy reality. I realized the culture of the Cougars football program had changed and we needed to get back to what was important. Change began at the top with me.

My staff had gotten complacent too, spending more time behind closed doors than with the players. I sat them down and emphasized the importance of being accessible to each other and especially to the players. That meant keeping office doors open and creating a welcoming environment. I met individually with each coach over the winter after the 2014 season, and engaged in some deep and frank discussions to root out problems and put all issues out on the table. You can't deal with things you're ignoring or hiding so we had a lot of difficult conversations.

I wanted my coaches to take a more hands-on approach. Meet with the players on a more regular basis; get to know them both as a team and as individuals. I wanted the coaching staff to know the players' dreams, desires, problems, and every challenge in their lives. That was the only way we could truly understand the team and thus encourage and motivate each young man to reach his potential.

I also started bringing everyone together for workouts in the weight room. My players, my coaches, and I met three times a week at 5:25 am to work out. We focused on learning how to lift weights correctly down to the minutest detail. In that weight room they were learning the basics of football all over again—following all directions from your coach, do everything you're instructed to do, do it right, and do it to your absolute best. By training as a group they'd not only encourage one another but also be inspired to work harder in front of their teammates. Everything done was for all to see and know. The successes, the effort, the results—there were no secrets.

Throughout that long, cold Indiana winter we worked out as a team both indoors and out. We endured together. We got to know each other better. And in the end we each strove to improve individually and as a team. Through those long days the team developed a new sense of purpose and lit a renewed fire under their desire to work together and win.

By the time we hit the field in the fall the culture had changed. The returning veterans were motivated by the disappointment of the 2014 season. They knew they had been a talented team that never reached its potential and they were determined to change that.

All that required group time in the weight room, which had in years before seen a lackluster attendance and participation spilled over into spring drills. That can-do spirit infected the new players coming in during summer camp and fueled an excitement at the start of the new season.

2015 turned into a magical year. It ended on a sour note, but that couldn't take away from what had been accomplished and what the future might yet deliver. Nor could it change the attitude of the rejuvenated Cougars.

We opened at home against Olivet Nazarene on September 5, 2015. Almost immediately after receiving the opening kick-off we scored on a seventy-nine-yard pass from sophomore quarterback Nick Ferrer to Cam Smith. The team never looked back. Despite a couple of fumbles the Cougars rolled to a 59-16 win.

Our game against Taylor in Upland the next week was an execution in perfection in the first half giving us a commanding 35-7 lead. By the time we were at 48-7 in third quarter I had pulled the first string and sent in the backups for some play experience.

Unexpectedly, Taylor refused to give up. They gave it all they had and by the fourth they had narrowed our once commanding lead to just six points at 48-42 with 3:30 still on the clock. I sent the first string back in and when junior defensive back NiShawn Lewis intercepted a Taylor pass with two minutes left in the game the tide was turned in our favor.

We went on to beat Trinity International 45-3 and Lindenwood Belleville 74-13 before encountering our biggest challenge of that season against archrival Marian. The number six Knights had been rated number one before their unexpected defeat at the hands of Robert Morris (IL) in Chicago the week before.

At the time, we were rated number eleven and were undefeated. The game didn't start well for us. Marian scored three times and led 21-0 before we finally got on the board at the end of the first quarter. In the second Marian scored early to take a substantial 28-7 lead. It looked as though it was going to be a long day for the Cougars. However, I could see the momentum in my guys shift as they came together as a unit and scored three times in the last half of the second quarter. By the half we had narrowed the score to 28-25. The icing on that cake was a nifty Ferrer handoff to Cody Appenzeller who then made a short jump pass to P.J. Dean in the end zone.

The third quarter was a repeat of what happened in the first. Marian came back from the half and seemed to reassert control scoring twice to take a 42-25 lead heading into the final quarter. I knew my guys were far from throwing in the towel and letting the Knights have their way. P.J. Dean made a forty-five-yard run at the 12:52 mark and with the extra point brought the score to 42-32. Ferrer followed that with a twenty-three-yard pass to Sean Boswell, getting us to 42-38 with 3:32 remaining.

The Knights converted on a third and twenty-seven that would have taken all the wind out of another team but not the Cougars. Defender Christian Johnson recovered an improbable Marian fumble on a short pitchout at midfield. Four plays later Boswell caught a Ferrer pass between the one and two-yard lines and somehow pushed two defenders over the goal line to put us in the lead for the first time. Ryan Nix added the extra point and just like that the Cougars led 45-42 with a minute left. Sophomore defender Lee Stewart intercepted a Knight desperation pass and it was over. Saint Francis had beaten its biggest rival and nemesis on their own turf. We had played our best game against better talent and come out ahead. That victory set the tone for the rest of the season.

We defeated Sienna Heights 49-25 the next week and Concordia 48-7 following that. The next opponent, Robert Morris (IL) had been the first team to upset Marian, and they fielded a formidable defense.

The game was as tough as I had expected it to be. We scored first but Robert Morris came back and scored twice in the second quarter to take a 14-7 lead at the half. In the third quarter we made the right plays and outscored the hosts to take a slim 24-22 lead going into the final quarter. We held a narrow 31-29 lead until NiShawn Lewis intercepted a pass and scored, giving us a 38-29 victory.

A scheduling issue led to playing a game with College of Faith that didn't count. The lopsided 61-0 score hides the level of mercy we provided the other team by keeping the clock running, shortening the quarters, and playing reserves.

The next week we completed the regular season with a 64-6 rout of Missouri Baptist. At the end of 2015 we were undefeated and had added another MSFA MEL championship to our resume.

The opening round of the NAIA playoffs pitted number four Saint Francis against number thirteen Reinhardt University from Waleska, Georgia. The Eagles were 9-1, used the triple-option offense, and averaged almost 55 points per game. We knew going in that we were going to have some serious competition.

In a near repeat of what happened in 2013 against Faulkner, another school from the deep south, snow started falling soon after the opening kickoff. It affected how both teams played. But we had been here before and we were determined to see a different outcome. We built a 24-7 halftime lead and led 37-14 at the end of the third. Reinhardt added their final points with 10 clicks left on the clock but it wasn't enough and we walked away with the win at 37-26.

In the quarterfinals we went up against number five Montana Tech. The Ore Diggers came out strong and scored after taking the opening kickoff down the field for a quick score. It took our guys a bit to adjust but they scored later in the first and again at the beginning of the second to open a 14-7 lead.

Just before the end of the half, a long pass from Ferrer to Seth Coate fell short and was intercepted. After that Montana Tech tied the score at 14. Our next two drives were cut off by thoughtless penalties, but we were slowly gaining control of the line of scrimmage on both sides of the ball and the clock was ticking.

In the half-time coaches meeting the coaching team made two adjustments regarding how we would line up to block on offense and send receivers over the middle that was being left open. In the third quarter these adjustments paid dividends as the Cougars had successful drives of ninety-five and ninety-eight yards bringing the score to 28-14. Montana Tech began to panic and that led to an interception, a touchdown from us, and a fumble on the kickoff that led to another touchdown to put the game out of reach for them. We dominated the second half to win 42-20 and advance to the semifinals for the first time since 2008.

After winning that dramatic come-from-behind 45-42 game in Indianapolis against Marian in early October we were feeling confident when we faced the Knights again on our home turf. We were one win away from playing for a national championship. I felt like we were back—back to where we had been from 2003-2008 when we made five straight appearances in the semifinals and played in three consecutive championships—and now we were poised to finally hit that national stage.

There was an overflowing crowd at D'Arcy Stadium for the first time since the beginning of 2014. In the pre-game warm-up drills Marian was quiet, focused, and all business. While we had been focusing on completing an undefeated season, Marian had been focusing on how to beat us, should we end up meeting again in the playoffs.

Since their back-to-back losses early in the year to Robert Morris and Saint Francis the Knights had buckled down. Their defense had smothered and squashed all their remaining opponents as their offense had churned out touchdowns led by their multipurpose player Krishawn Hogan.

Marian scored first but we tied the score at 7 all early in the second quarter, and it looked for an instant that it was going to be a classic contest. But after forcing Marian to settle for a field goal to bring the score to 10-7 the bottom literally fell out.

We fumbled the ball on the next series well in our own territory, which ended up giving the Knights excellent field position and an easy score followed by an avalanche of mistakes on our part and strong play that put Marian up 31-7 at halftime. By the end of the game the Knights' Hogan had scored six touchdowns, five rushing and one receiving against the Cougars. We couldn't seem to find a way to stop him.

It was a 45-14 whipping that stung and would be a source of motivation through the long cold winter to come. We did not play well that day. Marian definitely played better.

The pain of that defeat was softened slightly by Nick Ferrer being named MSFA MEL Offensive Player of the Year. I was named MSFA MEL Coach of the Year for the 10th time. But as I accepted that award, I looked around at all the people who had supported this team, all the players who had worked so hard, and vowed we wouldn't make the same mistakes again.

The 2016 Season

We spent another winter working diligently and another spring completing drill after drill. We had something to prove and we weren't ready to give up.

The 2016 opening game at Trinity International in Deerfield, Illinois provided some early tests. When we played there in 2011 the field was covered with slippery, smelly goose droppings. This time the grass was at least six inches tall, which negates speed and makes receivers running patterns more difficult. The grass slowed us down some but didn't change the outcome. We recorded a 34-20 win.

The following week we traveled to Bourbonnais, Illinois to play Olivet Nazarene. This time we got our offense going from the start and came away with a 58-14 victory. Our home opener against Taylor was a crushing loss for the other team. After a 24-0 lead in the beginning we cruised to a 37-6 win. The next Saturday we celebrated Homecoming with a 63-7 win over Lindenwood Belleville. We were 4-0, 2-0 in conference and anticipating meeting Marian.

Marian was rated number one and Saint Francis number two at that time. Our boys were eager to even the score and gain revenge for the 45-14 loss in the last year's NAIA semifinals. Going into that game the hype was over the top and the expectations were high. The crowd at D'Arcy Stadium was the largest of the season, but still far below what had been normal just a couple years before.

Marian started the scoring on a two-yard run with Krishawn Hogan. It was the first of three touchdowns he added to the six he had scored against the Cougars in last year's semifinal. We tied the game early in the second quarter on a Harris two-yard run.

The Knights answered with Hogan's second touchdown on a one-yard run to lead 14-7. We held the Knights there, and on the next possession Ferrer found Coate and connected on a thirty-eight-yard pass to tie the score at 14. As soon as we got the ball back we scored again, putting us ahead 21-14 at halftime.

The second half began with high hopes but after trading the ball back and forth Marian put a drive together that ended with a touchdown that tied the score with five minutes left in the third. The Knights took the lead early in the fourth quarter and slammed the door on us winning when Hogan scored a third touchdown with a little less than seven minutes remaining in the game. When it was all over we came up short again, losing 35-21. That game we were still trying to find ourselves and didn't play well.

Team morale was down the next week when we went up against Siena Heights in Adrian, Michigan. We led 21-10 at the half but in the second half the team began to lose steam.

Normally reliable Ryan Nix missing two field goal attempts at 41 and 31 yards.

Siena Heights scored in the third but missed the point after to trail 21-16. They scored again in the fourth on a fifty-eight-yard pass, failed to make the extra point, but had the lead at 22-21 with 6:48 on the clock. After getting the ball back Ferrer guided a twelve-play fifty-seven-yard drive to set up Nix's twenty-six yard field goal with 2:26 remaining. We pulled off a narrow 24-22 victory.

We returned to Michigan the following week to take on Concordia in Ann Arbor. After the close call with Siena Heights I made some adjustments to the offense to get more balance.

Nevertheless the first half was close. Saint Francis led 10-6 and gave up two field goals. The second half was a different story. The offensive changes finally settled in and this, I think, became the real turning point of the Cougars' 2016 season. The boys came out the second half and dominated, scoring four touchdowns in the third quarter to take a commanding 38-6 lead and adding a final TD in the fourth to walk off with a 44-6 win.

Our running game that day was a big part of the team's success. That year I had three running backs that looked like Heisman candidates: Justin Green (96 yards), Aaron Harris (87 yards), and P.J. Dean (66 yards). Nick Ferrer passed for 225 of Saint Francis's 474 yards.

But that was only half the story. Our defense held the other teams accountable and was a dominant group who controlled the line of scrimmage.

The next Saturday we faced our final big test of the season against number twenty-four Robert Morris (IL). They were one of the toughest teams we faced during the regular season and the game turned into a nail biter. Robert Morris scored first midway through the first quarter and held the lead until Sean Boswell caught Nick Ferrer's pass, despite interference, sitting on the turf in the end zone with less than a minute remaining in the half. That tied the score.

We added two more scores in the third quarter to take a 21-7 lead going into the fourth. Robert Morris wasn't ready to go quietly however. They put a score on the board in the first half of the fourth bringing them to 21-14, but we answered that with another touchdown. Robert Morris mounted a drive that brought them within reach, trailing 28-21 with almost seven minutes left.

After getting the ball back Robert Morris completed a long pass that gave them a first and goal situation sitting on the one-yard line. Three plays later they were on the three after our defense stopped Kenyatte Allen, the Eagles quarterback, on a bootleg play that had worked for them all day. That goal line stand prevented Robert Morris from scoring and either beating us or sending us into overtime.

We finished the regular season with a 56-24 win over Missouri Baptist and a 35-6 win over Davenport in Grand Rapids, Michigan. 2016 ended on a high with us posting a 9-1 record.

Our first challenge in the NAIA playoffs was number eleven Missouri Valley. True to recent tradition the day was cold with a stiff wind out of the north as the sky changed from dark clouds to sun and back again. It started snowing early in the game, but the flakes didn't persist. Saint Francis' persistence was another matter.

After a forty-five-minute first quarter that ended with us holding a slim 21-20 lead the snow diminished. We were just getting started. The team powered forward leading 44-20 at the half 65-20 at the end of three and 79-20 at the end. It was a performance to put all future adversaries on notice. We had finally found ourselves and the team's confidence zoomed.

The quarterfinal match up pitted number four Saint Francis against number five Morningside from Sioux City, Iowa. They were the best team we played that season, and they really made us work for every point.

We were down 20-0 in the second quarter but managed to finally get on the board with 44 seconds left on an eleven-yard pass from Ferrer to Coate. We scored twice in the third to take a 21-20 lead before Morningside scored and added a two-point conversion to lead 28-21 going into the final quarter.

That's when things came together for the Cougars. All that hard work, all the practice, all the team building and speeches coalesced. We scored three times adding twenty-one points to lead 42-28 with a little more than two minutes left. Morningside came back and scored to make it 42-35, but the ensuing onside kickoff attempt failed and after we gained a critical first down the game was over. It was a great comeback, an incredible game to coach and to see. That win marked my 300th career victory as a college football coach.

It seemed hard to believe that I had reached that milestone. It didn't seem that long ago that I couldn't find a job anywhere—and here I was celebrating multiple seasons as a winning coach. There was just something special about the magic at Saint Francis that had a lot to do with getting me to that point.

The greatly anticipated and desired rematch with Marian in the semifinals didn't take place. Undefeated number one Marian met with unexpected difficulty in their quarterfinal game with number nine Southern Oregon and was eliminated in a 17-0 game played at home. Marian's loss meant Saint Francis would go to Waleska, Georgia to face undefeated number three Reinhardt instead.

We had faced Reinhardt in the opening round the year before and that gave us some valuable insights into their game play. We stepped onto the field as the underdog. To me that wasn't a bad thing. It was another adversity—and another chance for us to overcome.

Reinhardt felt their loss to Saint Francis in 2015 had been largely due to weather. It snowed during that game and our Indiana-based Cougars had adapted more readily to the environment than the team from Georgia. This time, in their eyes, it was going to be different. Saint Francis was playing in their yard and the temperature was in the upper 50s so there was nothing there that would help Saint Francis—or so Reinhardt hoped and believed.

Reinhardt took a 7-0 lead late in the first quarter, but our guys answered right back with three touchdowns in the second with Justin Green running for two and Seth Coate adding the third on a thirty-two-yard pass from Ferrer. Reinhardt added a field goal as time expired and Saint Francis went into the dressing room leading 21-10.

In the third quarter the two teams alternated touchdowns bringing the score to 28-17. Just when it looked as if we were going to lose our momentum our defense stepped up. Marcus Stepp intercepted a pass and took it thirty yards into the end zone to add some breathing room by giving Saint Francis a 35-17 advantage.

In the fourth quarter, another Ferrer to Coate pass covering thirty-four yards put us ahead with a commanding 42-17 score. Reinhardt managed one more touchdown, but it wasn't enough. Saint Francis won, 42-24.

That was the moment we had all been working forever since I first arrived in Fort Wayne, Indiana. We were heading to the national championship for the first time in ten years.

Two weeks later we were in Daytona Beach, Florida for the game on December 17th. Most of the media attention was focused on our opponent Baker University from Baldwin City, Kansas. Baker averaged fifty points a game led by Logan Brettell who had been awarded the NAIA Player of the Year at the annual Champions of Character banquet the night before. Brettell had thrown for 4800 yards and 51 touchdowns and was aided by three receivers/running backs that had each gained over 1000 yards.

Our defense took note, and was prepared to stop them. Baker took the opening kick-off and promptly marched down the field, but the drive stalled when our defense held fast. Baker had to settle for a twenty-six-yard field goal. We returned the kickoff across the 40 to set up a good field position. Justin

Green had one great carry but the next two gained little creating a fourth and one situation at our own 48. Logic says this early in the game the best option is to kick.

I didn't listen to logic.

My team lined up to go for the first down. Most of the people in the stadium were wondering what on earth Saint Francis was doing. The ball was given to Nicodemus to run off tackle. He found a wide hole and was able to not only pick up the first down but also carry the ball to the Baker two-yard line before he was caught. That run set up our first touchdown. That moment of total dominance made our confidence skyrocket.

That call was the play that turned the game. Baker never really recovered due in part to a lot of inspired defensive play by the Cougars. In the course of a long season where they had been burned a few times the passing defense was at its best and the pressure on Baker's Brettell was unrelenting. He was sacked, pressured, and hurried, resulting in five interceptions.

We led 17-3 at the half. In the third quarter after a Baker scored narrowed the lead to 17-10, we responded and brought the score to 24-10. At the beginning of the fourth quarter we increased that margin to 31-10 before Baker cut the lead to 31-17 with 3:39 to go.

P.J. Dean completed scoring on a twenty-eight-yard run with 2:48 left. We held onto the ball for those last two minutes and then, it was over. I stood there stunned for a moment as I realized what had just happened.

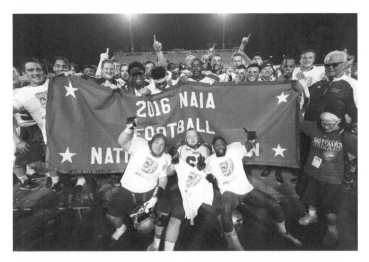

Coach Donley, Sister Elise, and team raise
2016 Championship Banner.

Nineteen years ago I had promised the University of Saint Francis, their supporters, and a whole lot of naysayers that this football team would be national champions.

In that stadium in Florida on a warm December evening we had done it. We had won the national championship.

I can't even begin to describe the celebration afterwards. The team was just as shocked and overjoyed as I was. There was a new level of school pride when we returned to Fort Wayne and a groundswell of support that surpassed all we had seen before.

We started with nothing, and nineteen years later we had secured one national championship, played in the final game four times, lost in the playoffs to the winner or runner up twelve times, and lost to the eventual national champion nine times. Not a bad record for a program that started with little more than some hope, a converted semi trailer, and a stone-filled field.

When I got back home to Fort Wayne the school honored me by extending my contract through 2021. It was icing on the cake. I love what I do and I'll keep on doing it as long as they let me.

The 2017 Season

Winning a national championship is not easy and trying to repeat that feat is even more daunting. At the awards banquet after winning the 2016 championship Fort Wayne Mayor Tom Henry said to me, "You think this one was difficult wait until 2017. The target will be on your back in the regular season and you'll face tough competition in the postseason." His prediction was a pretty good description of our 2017 season.

We opened the season by taking a long bus ride to the University of Jamestown in Jamestown, North Dakota. They were starting a new program and we had an open date. We came back home after thrashing them 55-7. That game provided us with a chance to test some things and see where we were. We followed that up with an impressive 68-23 crushing of the University of Saint Francis (IL) team in our home opener. We followed that up with a 49-21 victory over rival Saint Ambrose in Davenport, Iowa.

We returned home the following week to face perennial rival Saint Xavier in a night game. It was also homecoming so many of our former players were back to watch. They weren't disappointed. Ferrer was on target, our receivers executed their routes and caught passes, and Justin Green piled up yards on the ground as we whipped them 48-23. Saint Xavier was undefeated at that point and rated fifth in the NAIA rankings, and already owned a win over our next opponent number eight rated Marian.

We knew going to Indianapolis to face Marian would be challenging regardless what records or statistics suggested and we were right. The target was firmly affixed to our backs and Marian was keyed up and ready. It turned out to be our tightest contest of the regular season. Marian scored first and had a 14-0 lead before we got things going. We finally got on the scoreboard but trailed 24-17 at the half. Being down had no effect on us. We knew what we had to do and were confident we could do it. In the second half we went out and tied the game in the third at 24-24 and scored with a bit more than six minutes left in the fourth to lead 31-24. Then the defense took over. They made a strong statement by shutting Marian's offense down in the second half.

Things were not going to get any easier. Saint Ambrose, Saint Xavier, and Marian were all highly rated opponents and returning home the next week we faced our fourth consecutive rated opponent. Concordia came into the game undefeated and wanting to make a point and send the Cougars a message. The Cardinals had a solid defense and demonstrated it by stopping Saint Francis on two consecutive drives deep in the red zone without giving up a point.

I probably should have settled for kicking field goals, but we went for it instead and they stopped us. Concordia got some unexpected help in both cases when receivers Sean Boswell and Dan Ricksy, who were usually flawless, dropped passes in the end zone. Concordia took an early 8-0 lead but successive touchdown drives with scores by Justin Green gave us a slim 12-8 halftime lead.

Saint Francis added a field goal early in the third to go up 15-8, but Concordia answered on the next series to tie the score at 15. On their next possession Concordia took the lead with a field goal to lead 18-15 after three quarters. But that lead wasn't to endure. We came right back and added a field goal at the opening of the final quarter to tie the score again at 18. Gavin Gardner added another field goal on our next drive to give Saint Francis the lead for good with just under seven minutes remaining, to go up 21-18.

No one could have written a better script for what happened next. We traded the ball back and forth until our cornerback

Ryan Johnson recovered a fumble and returned it 46 yards to give the Cougars a 28-18 advantage with 3:36 remaining.

It was very windy that day with 30mph gusts blowing south to north. We caught the Cardinals a bit by surprise on the ensuing kickoff. We executed a short high kick toward the Cougar sidelines and the wind held the ball up long enough for a host of Cougars to be waiting for it to come down. We were able to get possession well into Cardinal territory. A play or two later Justin Green broke loose on the right side and sprinted twenty-six yards to give us a comfortable 35-18 lead after Gardner kicked the point after and sealed the victory.

It had been a tough stretch with adverse circumstances. We dug in and prevailed, but not without cost. One of our key receivers sophomore Rocky James went out late in the first half with a leg injury that would keep him off the field until the playoffs.

Saint Francis cruised through the next three games with relatively easy victories over Siena Heights, Missouri Baptist, and Lindenwood Belleville.

The final game of the regular season against rival Taylor was a mixed blessing of sorts. Junior running back Justin

Green scored four touchdowns including a 96-yard kickoff return to begin the game. QB Nick Ferrer threw a touchdown pass to Dan Ricksy in the first half, his 127th career touchdown pass, extending the MSFA record. On the dark side we had an uncharacteristic three fumbles lost, an interception in the end zone, and a missed extra point.

It was a strange game. We had more turnovers than we'd had all season. It was a kind of a sloppy game, but we probably needed one to learn from. We finished the regular season 10-0. Undefeated seasons aren't easy to come by with our schedule.

Because we had an open date at the end of our schedule we had two weeks to get everyone healthy and prepared for our first playoff opponent on November 18th. We drew Benedictine College from Atchison, Kansas.

Everything cooperated except the weather. On Saturday morning it was warm and wet. The sky opened and dumped as much as six inches of rain in some locations. The teams started their warm-up drills in a downpour of near epic proportions, but lightning interrupted midway through it. The teams left the field and the rain continued.

After a meeting and consultation between AD's from Saint Francis and Benedictine, the respective coaches, officials, and the NAIA office, it was determined that the game would be delayed until 6:00 pm to give the dangerous lightning and most of the rain time to pass. It was still going to be wet and the temperature was going to be falling, but the game would be played. More importantly players would be safe from lightning and we would still be on schedule.

By game time there was a steady, heavy, misty rain that continued until the very end of the game. After kicking off to Benedictine Saint Francis took over on downs. With Ferrer at the helm the Cougars methodically marched down the field and scored to take a 6-0 lead. The extra point was blocked and the score remained unchanged until late in the first half when Benedictine connected on a long pass to put them in position to tie the score and with the point after take a 7-6 lead. Getting the ball back at their own forty-four-yard line after we failed to convert on a fourth down and three Benedictine was able to add another seven points just before half-time.

The locker room was quiet as the players gathered themselves. They were confident in their abilities. All they had to do was execute. When they came back on the field for the second half, they did. Justin Green took the opening kickoff eighty-six yards to cut the deficit to two and Nick Ferrer threw a two-point conversion to Ricksy to tie the score at 14. From there Saint Francis defense took over and forced Benedictine into three consecutive three and outs while adding another score for Saint Francis to retake the lead for good at 20-14. This time the snap on the point after was bobbled in the wet conditions.

Saint Francis added another touchdown on an eleven-yard snag by senior Zach Gegner. The two-point attempt failed, but the Cougars led 26-14 with 8:55 left. Benedictine was not about to go quietly. They mounted another attack and connected on a thirty-five-yard pass and with the extra point trailed 26-21 with 6:50 still to be played.

We were forced to give the ball up with over three minutes left on the clock giving Benedictine another chance. This time the defense stiffened and when junior cornerback Stan Jackson stepped in front of the ball on a fourth down attempt Benedictine's hopes faded and we sealed the win.

In the quarterfinals, Saint Francis faced Northwestern Iowa a team with an offense averaging 37 points a game. They had just beaten number seven Langston in Oklahoma 55-7 the previous week.

It was a day for defense. We held a slim 7-3 lead until sophomore free safety Blake Schumacher intercepted a pass and returned it to give us good field position deep in Northwestern Iowa territory. We were able to convert the opportunity into points when Ferrer completed a fourteen-yard pass to Dan Ricksy in the end zone with seconds remaining. Up to that point the Cougars had been sputtering with Ferrer being sacked four times, giving up an interception, a muffed punt return, and at least two uncharacteristic dropped passes.

The second half was a different game. The defense came out strong and stopped the Red Raiders cold, forcing repeated three and outs. The defense made two key interceptions, forced a fumble, and made a defining goal line stand late in the game by holding Northwestern out of the end zone after having a first down and goal and maybe a foot-and-a-half.

The 30-3 final score showed the defense was maturing and getting better and raising their level of play, which helped get our offense back in sync.

One of those little intangibles that are hard to calculate and quantify could be attributed to junior cornerback Stan Jackson. Jackson's energy and enthusiasm is infectious. He made a key knockdown on a pass on a fourth down that ended any hope of Benedictine upsetting the Cougars the week before. That energy continued to build after the game and into the next week.

Jackson and running back Justin Green came up with the idea of having a turnover chain (something the Miami Hurricanes break out to celebrate each of their takeaways). Jackson borrowed a chain necklace from his mother and modified it by adding the Saint Francis logo. The chain arrived just in time for the Northwestern Iowa game and Jackson literally pulled it out and introduced it to the rest of the team a few minutes before kickoff.

It didn't take long for Jackson to get the whole defense hyped up. Maybe it was coincidence, but we intercepted three passes, recovered a fumble, made several key stops, and forced

Northwestern into having to punt from its own end zone twice. The idea was each time a defensive player made a key play and forced a turnover he got to wear the chain. It was fitting that Jackson got to wear the chain after knocking down and then intercepting a pass in the end zone that ended the last Northwestern Iowa scoring threat.

Chain or not we ended up having a good day. The Cougars limited the Red Raiders to 57 yards on the ground, far below the more than 400 they had put up the week before.

The semi-final playoff brought together perhaps the two best teams in the NAIA. Morningside (Iowa) entered the day undefeated with a 13-0 record, and an impressive list of lopsided wins over the course of the 2017 season. The Mustangs were rated number three.

The Cougars came out fast and furious to start the game. They took the opening kickoff and marched methodically down the field and scored. We went on to build a 19-3 lead but at some cost. Kicker Gavin Gardner suffered a hip injury kicking the first extra point and had to leave the game. A bit later receiver Rocky James came down on the side of his ankle trying to catch a pass on the Saint Francis sideline and had to leave the game.

Donley, Sister Elise, and the Saint Francis team celebrate winning back-to-back championships with the 2017 National Championship trophy.

We built a lead but Morningside was far from finished. The Mustangs put together a drive late in the second period that closed the margin to 19-10 at halftime. In the third Morningside scored to make the score 19-17, but the Cougars answered with a four-yard pass from Ferrer to Boswell capping a nine-play, seventy-yard drive to make it 25-17. Morningside answered back with a 39-yard field goal to close the gap to 25-20.

Morningside took their only lead of the game near the beginning of the fourth capped with a two-point conversion to take a 28-25 lead. The lead was brief. Justin Green took a handoff from Ferrer on the next series less than a minute later and found some wiggle room through middle of Morningside's defense and sprinted the remaining sixty-one yards untouched to put Saint Francis back on top to stay at 31-28.

Morningside had the opportunity to regain the lead or tie the game, but the Cougar defense stopped the Mustangs and forced a nineteen-yard field goal attempt on fourth down. The snap from center was mishandled and the kick was low and the slim lead preserved. Saint Francis then moved the ball 80 yards in eight plays, again capped by Justin Green's nineteen-yard run to give us some breathing room and a 37-28 lead with 3:53 left.

Morningside wasn't giving up, but defensive cornerback Stan Jackson stepped in front of the Morningside quarterback's pass and somehow managed to weave his way through the defense to find the end zone and give us what looked like an insurmountable 43-28 lead with 59 seconds left. Still Morningside would not concede. The Mustangs took the ball down the field and with a two-point conversion trailed only 43-36 with 17 seconds left.

The Mustangs attempted an onside kick, but Saint Francis was prepared. Senior Sean Boswell grabbed the ball and held on in the ensuing pile of players that resulted.

The Cougars prevailed in a very different and difficult victory. Without a kicker we were forced to go for the two-point conversion after each score and failed on each try. Usually when you give up six extra points in a tough game the result isn't in your favor, but we prevailed and showed we were ready to defend our championship.

Reinhardt came into the championship undefeated and led by a first-year coach in the fifth year of the school's football program. They were ranked number two and possessed a formidable defense and a powerful ground game on offense. We had more experience and a more rounded offense that included All-American running back Justin Green, NAIA Player of the Year Quarterback Nick Ferrer, a well seasoned receiver corps, and a talented and experienced defense.

We were fortunate early after a missed handoff from Ferrer to Green was fumbled and picked up by a Reinhardt defender who then had the ball stripped away by Green and recovered by Saint Francis. After being stopped and forced to kick on fourth down Reinhardt's punt receiver fumbled and we recovered at the Reinhardt thirty-yard line. We weren't able to turn that into a touchdown, but we put three on the board with Gardner's field goal.

Reinhardt took the kickoff and advanced but the drive was thwarted and they missed the ensuing thirty-yard field goal attempt giving the ball back to us.

Over the next several minutes Saint Francis would do all the damage necessary to Reinhardt to win the football game. Justin Green took a handoff from Ferrer and found a hole to take the ball eighty yards for the score, and Gardner's point after was perfect to make it 10-0 Cougars. That was followed with another score on a sixteen-yard pass from Ferrer to Blackwell as the first quarter wound down to make it 17-0.

The Cougars topped off their scoring on their next drive that ended with Justin Green's second touchdown on a ten-yard scamper around the right side. Gardner's kick made it 24-0. Halfway through the second quarter Reinhardt got on the board and with the extra point trailed 24-7 at the half.

Reinhardt made some adjustments to their defense at the half and coupled with the losses of senior inside receiver Shawn Boswell and sophomore inside receiver Duke Blackwell to injuries the offense sputtered in the second half.

Reinhardt was able to put a successful drive together and added a score with a bit over five minutes remaining in the third, but a Saint Francis defender got a hand on the kick and the Saint Francis lead was cut to 24-13. But we held that lead and that became the final score.

Saint Francis became the first school to repeat as champions since the University of Sioux Falls won back-to-back titles in 2008-2009. Only five schools have accomplished winning back-to-back championships including Carroll College's four-peat in 2002-2005.

We have a great sense of accomplishment, but we're not finished. Every year brings us new challenges, and new chances to show the world what we've got.

PART THREE

POST-GAME LESSONS

Chapter 13

Facing Adversity Off the Field

There are many different aspects to overcoming adversity. In building a successful college football program from the ground up some of the most significant challenges faced are not on the field. There's a game that's played under the stadium lights and another one played in the shadows outside of the field.

Every player and coach would love it if the football program received total support every day of the year, but the reality is that not all faculty or administrators have the same enthusiasm. In their defense they have their own projects and visions for the future of the university. Sometimes that includes football, sometimes it doesn't.

A football program requires a pretty sizable financial contribution both during the season and off-season. There's the buildings, equipment, travel costs, but there's also recruitment, scholarships, staff, training. Then there's advertising and marketing—all dollars that are spent on an annual basis with the hope that the investment will yield a favorable return.

Not all teams win. And some that do don't necessarily make a lot of money for the university. The public can be fickle—there when you are on a winning streak, but leaving empty seats when you suffer a loss or two. That's when the bean counters look at the numbers and start wondering why the school is supporting something that isn't bringing in revenue.

In the years I have been a coach I have faced a lot of challenges from well-meaning faculty and administrators. It's the part of the job no one tells you about when you're standing on the field with your first group of sweaty, eager players. At that point, all a coach is thinking about is the team and the game. But neglecting the bureaucratic part of the job can cost the best coach a lot more than he or she expected. Adversity is always your companion.

Some people in the university see athletics and football in particular as a plum they might pick, as if they could remove its funding and contractual obligations from the branches of the school budget.

When I was serving as Athletic Director not all of the changes I instituted were met with hearty approval. There was some argument that being Athletic Director and football coach was a conflict of interest. In my case I was not contractually bound to both positions, but in every decision I made I was doing the best for both the program and the school.

Ultimately, I stepped down as AD and recruited an experienced athletic director who had been at IPFW, and had helped lead the school's move to Division I status in all sports. He brought his own ideas to the athletic program at Saint Francis, including a decision to raise the bar for academic requirements for students in the athletics program. He thought they should be higher than what the National Association Intercollegiate Athletics (NAIA) required. I had some issues with this change, mostly because I knew having worked with the student athletes for so many years that this wasn't a change to make lightly.

The national organization allowed a student athlete a year to adjust to college life and raise their grade point average (GPA) to a minimum level. For the last fifty years the NAIA required student athletes to have a minimum 1.8 grade point average by the time they completed 24 credit hours of college work in order to compete in the next season, and a 2.0 grade point average to graduate from college.

The policy change was to be put into place in April. I went to the AD and told him I was concerned the change would be too hasty for several reasons. First, sometimes student players get bad academic advice and get put into courses they shouldn't be in. Second, there is a big adjustment from high school to college. And third, it can take a good semester or two for a student to adjust to the demands of both college classes and team duties.

My concerns were ignored and the new rule was implemented and put into place after students had gone home for the summer. It was an immediate requirement with no grandfather clause, which meant any student athlete who had gone home with a GPA too low wouldn't be able to play sports when he or she returned to school in the fall, at least not

180

without taking classes over the summer to raise their GPA. Not all students can afford the time or tuition to take summer classes, especially when those classes had to be taken at Saint Francis. Ultimately five members of our one hundred and seventy-member team were not able to meet the new standards.

Dealing with administrators can be a real challenge because they don't necessarily have the same goals and vision. My view is from within the football program. Theirs is from within their academic and administrative programs. It requires finesse and constant communication to make sure both sides of the school work together for the good of the university as a whole.

It helps a great deal when you have a committed leader who understands all sides of the university programs. Saint Francis President Sister Elise is a saint. She is an amazing leader— she delegates, then steps away and lets people run with their strengths.

Adversity often appears at times and in places we least expect, like in the offices of the university. Learning to deal with it and finding ways of turning those moments and instances into opportunity is one of life's most valuable lessons. A lesson we all must learn as we strive to become the best we can be.

Chapter 14

Building a Team Begins with Relationships and Trust

When I first arrived at USF to begin building a football program, we tried to recruit pretty much every warm body with a pulse and a high school diploma. I had a stack of names and phone numbers of potential players. I'd sit there in that little condemned shack converted for use as an office and make call after call.

One night I called a young man and when he answered, I went through my spiel: I'm Coach Donley, University of Saint Francis…. I went on for a couple minutes and I hear this kid say "Mom, I think it's a recording." That moment made me realize the people on my list weren't just names and numbers, they were real people who mattered. People who wanted to feel like they mattered. It changed every phone call I made after that.

The second component to finding a connection with the players is building trust in the relationship. They want to know that they can depend on you when they need help or when they're nervous or unsure. They want to know that you see them as more than a number on a field

When I first started coaching in my twenties I thought you had to treat everybody the same, but you don't because everybody is different. Success in coaching comes from learning the mental makeup of every coach and every player and then detecting what buttons to push to make them do their best. That will govern how you approach one player versus another, whether you use a firm or relaxed tone, or a combination of the two.

At a Saturday afternoon football game when these young men trust you and know you truly see them they are more receptive to the lessons that will hopefully teach them to become the best they can be.

Saint Francis won a lot of football games in 1999, 2000, and 2001. We weren't an especially good or talented team. Yes we had a couple of outstanding players, but most of the kids on the team were average guys. We didn't win because of some master strategy or one amazing quarterback. We won because we had a positive attitude.

Building that attitude is an all-year priority. It starts right after the season ends with season wrap-ups and goal setting. In the winter in the weight room there's another opportunity for team building and attitude adjustment. In the spring that attitude is easier to find because everyone's optimistic. After the first few days the kids get into the routine and start having fun. We try to promote optimism—and that means we, as coaches have to see the glass as half full and then find a way to fill it.

That means looking at each individual player and adapting our coaching strategy to suit the player not the other way around. I had one set of brothers who were polar opposites in personality. One played on defense, one played offense. But their personalities couldn't have been more different. What motivated one would have the opposite effect on the other. Every player is different and every approach is different.

We have team guidelines and we clearly draw the line in the sand with the players about our expectations. But motivation is a personal thing and to get each player to play at their best means finding out which buttons to hit. That means getting to know your players not just walking in to coach for a few hours and walking out again. It was one of the reasons I did the weight room workouts with the guys—I wanted to get to know them without the pressure of a practice or the distraction of a game.

At the beginning of every season I worry that the players might not be ready. There are so many unknowns and variables and outside factors that influence the boys on the team. To try to build a winning team we have to be very careful schematically to get the ball in the hands of the playmakers we have then hope and pray to God that some of the younger more inexperienced players develop into great players.

I try to build a team from the middle out— quarterback, tailback, and center. Getting to the finals means being just as effective running as throwing.

If a back gets the ball twenty-five times in an early-season game he might not be as prepared physically as he could be to deal with that so we make sure we protect him well and keep him out of situations where the opponents can get a shot at him. We build on their skills all season. Coaching a team is a continual ongoing process with parts shifting in and out of place game by game.

One of the things that the players don't realize is how much of football is a mental game. Sure it helps to be strong or fast, but the game requires continuously making the right choices and decisions on the field.

For the coaches, those decisions are ones that can affect young people's lives. Sometimes that means eliminating those players who still think it's all about them, and they haven't grasped the true concept of a team. If my best player is cutting class, coming to practice late, mouthing off and acting irresponsible, I'm going to cut him, regardless of how he plays on the field. The team as a whole is more important than a single component player. Cutting someone who is acting with clear disregard for the rules and expectations of the coach can be a valuable learning lesson for him and other players. They learn to deal with the consequences, to be responsible, and to make the effort to fulfill their commitment in the classroom and on the football field.

When I have had to do that in the past, I have seen a positive impact on the team. The rest of the players step up to fill the gap. It's about teaching them to make tough decisions. If the kids don't understand that they have a job to do, that they have a responsibility not to cut corners or shirk responsibilities, then we haven't done our job as coaches.

It takes some time. Those eighteen-year-old freshmen can come from privileged backgrounds or from schools that turned a blind eye to bad behavior. These kids don't necessarily understand commitment and hard work and what those two things mean to a team. My players earn the right to be on the team. It's not a given just because they can run the ball or pass it fifty yards.

An essential part of creating a successful team involves working with players to help them define themselves. When I first start talking with a player I ask him some basic questions about his future benchmarks: What are your goals? You want to be an All-American? You want to be All-Conference? You want to be a starter? Do you want to make the travel roster? Then I help them set goals that help them reach that potential.

Every kid coming into the program has at least a few of those goals. But there's also a level of reality they have to face that they might be great players but not excellent players. They have to understand the reality of their capabilities, what they can and cannot do better. I can count on one hand the number of players in my almost forty years of coaching who have gone on to play in the NFL.

However, we still want them to be the best they can be. Football isn't about ending up with the Packers or the Colts. It's about learning to reach your maximum potential on the field and in life.

On the opposite side you have players with tremendous potential who are underachievers. Sometimes you can find the key to igniting their drive and sometimes not.

I liken it to filling a bucket. The kids come in and they might have a huge bucket of talent, but it's not filled all the way because there are so many other things that go into filling it—teamwork, listening, focus. One year, I had a player come to see me who wanted more playing time on the team. He was the number two-ranked running back in the state and he told me he was bigger, stronger, faster and a better athlete than the guy playing ahead of him.

I had watched him on the field for a while and when I sat down with him I told him that he was right. He was bigger, stronger and faster, but his bucket was only half-filled. He made mental errors, came late to meetings and practice, and made countless mental errors because he had a limited attention span and didn't listen. I told him he wouldn't be a starter until he got those things under control and learned how to fill his bucket. It wasn't a physical issue, it was an efficiency issue—how efficient was he in all those other areas? Those are the things that will serve him well in the long run.

How you achieve it? Now where are you? Where you are at this time becomes your role.

Some players who are disappointed they don't get more playing time will exercise their option to leave while others will understand the bigger picture and start working harder. That's how it works in the real world once they leave this campus. Not everyone goes out and makes a million dollars. Not everyone reaches the top of his or her field. Not everyone lands in his or her dream career. They have to adapt, redirect, and reassess. Just like the best players do in practice and on the field. They perform consistently and never stop striving to be better.

Chapter 15

Winning, It's a Lot More Than Numbers on the Scoreboard

Win.

That's the word I hear most from administration, fans, players, parents—are we going to win the game? Are we going to win the championship? The win/loss ratio is the public face of the program and many people don't understand that what's important is the foundation of the team, which is designed to create strong and responsible young people not necessarily a winning team.

A car dealer, for example, can go through a day and not sell a single car and nobody knows or cares except him. On the other hand if my team falters on Saturday afternoon and we don't win everyone from coast-to-coast seems to know and has an opinion on why. I turned on the news one night and the first thing the sportscaster talked about was our loss to Carroll College in the 2007 semi-finals. Society puts all the emphasis and importance on winning the big game. Yes I wanted to beat Carroll College. Yes I wanted to win a national championship, and so did everybody in Fort Wayne, at the university, and every member of our coaching staff and team. The fact was Carroll might have been better, or at least they were in December 2007 on the frozen tundra out in Montana. The only thing we have control of is making sure we are doing the best we can.

When we won that national championship at Georgetown in 1991 I had most of the same team coming back the next year and people expected a repeat. But at the time I was forty years old and didn't have the experience on how to deal with success, on keeping the mindset, and also focusing on continual improvement in that day-to-day process. Georgetown finished the 1992 season with an 11-2 record, and I learned a lot about myself as a coach and about my goals off the field.

My job isn't to win—it's to teach these young people how to become the best they can be so they can leave that field and lead productive lives. I want to instill in these young people that they have to take the responsibility and initiative themselves to develop into good people, and understand that it's not all about succeeding.

Believe me nobody wants to win more than I do. But I know that no one succeeds in life all the time. Failures aren't necessarily failures—sometimes they are necessary steps along the path God has laid out for you. You might not see that until those failures are in your rearview mirror, but keeping the plan in mind helps make it easier to work through defeat. The only thing we have control over is how well we do our job, how much we give to the moment, and what kind of people we are.

Over the course of my career, I've studied a lot of other coaches. I've spent time with Woody Hayes (Ohio State), Bo Schembeckler (Michigan), and several other amazing coaches. I come back to their advice often, but it's Vince Lombardi's words that echo in my head every season. His famous quote, "Winning is the only thing" is interpreted as meaning winning on the scoreboard, but I see the meaning of his words a bit differently. To me winning is found in your everyday life. It's about being the best you can be all the time in all ways. Sometimes that carries through on the field, if you've got the arms and legs to back up the attitude, the effort, and the commitment. Sometimes what happens on the field carries over into everyday life. To me winning is about a lot more than numbers on the scoreboard.

Chapter 16

The Coat of Arms Process

In Medieval times the coat of arms was used to celebrate a family's history and to distinguish individuals. I do something similar with each new player at the beginning of summer camp. Doing this exercise helps kids sort out their priorities and focus on what is important.

We don't do this exercise every year so it doesn't become rote, but do it at least once with every player. I divide the players into groups of ten to twelve, then have them list their goals in every aspect of life: as a football player, as a student, and as a person. I ask them questions such as: What do you want to accomplish short range? Where do you want to be four years from now? Where do you want to be ten years from now? How are you going to accomplish those things? What needs to be done to accomplish your short-term goals, your intermediate goals, and your long-range goals? I also have them do this for academic and personal goals.

The groups are intentionally mixed to make sure they include upperclassman, underclassmen, and rookies. To encourage interaction, I assign a coach to each group to listen. There is a mixture of seniority among the players. Questions are devised that force discussion between them as it relates to team goals and how they are going to accomplish them. Sometimes they argue and sometimes they laugh until they cry. But they find common answers through these exercises.

The groups are then broken into four quadrants and are presented with a question they must work through as a group. They are asked to create and draw a symbol that best represents their consensus. The coaches then take the symbols created by each group, combine them, and make a coat of arms for the team. It helps us work on where we are going and how we are going to get there.

At this age many of these young people are focused on monetary goals. They have no idea of what they want to do in the future or have the slightest idea how to get there, just that they want to make a lot of money doing it. The first thing we try to accomplish is to get these kids to assess what's really important. Is it all about the money, or is it about doing the right things in life, living a good life, and feeling good about what you do? I ask them what kind of impact they want to leave in this world. When you're gone what do you want your family, friends, and your children to think about you? Getting them to answer these questions helps them decide how they should gear their lives.

So many kids say, "I want to go to the NFL. I want to be famous." They have no idea what all that entails. They need to be able to evaluate themselves, know their strengths and appreciate their limitations. It's all about setting realistic goals—long-range, personally, and team.

I tell the kids that you have to have an idea of where you want to go otherwise you're going to head down the road and end up lost or somewhere completely apart from your goals and dreams. My goal was to work as a coach in South Bend. I ended up only 90 miles away doing a job that I love.

This exercise creates a web of connection and shared vision. Any time you have a business or a team where there are nearly two hundred people involved, from players to staff, you have to find a way to interweave them so that we are all working toward the same future. We start with the small goals and work up: The first week of camp, where do we want to be at physically? The first week of class, what do we want to accomplish? What do we need do for first game week prep? How do we prepare for the first big challenge? Where do we want to be at the end of the season?

Throughout the year, we come back to the coat of arms by asking the players where are we as an organization? We can then assess and shift to meet those new demands and challenges.

As the group gets into talking about long-range personal goals there is a reflection of the social-economic status and environments each of these players brings with him. Some players come from very wealthy backgrounds. Sometimes those kids have been spoiled, but other times they come from families with high expectations. The parent with control of the checkbook expects a certain level of achievement. Maybe their parents were hard on them their whole lives, and for some, coming here gives them a feeling of serenity. They can concentrate on the game instead of everything going on back home. It's the same for the kids from the poorer backgrounds. Everyone on the team is an equal, and with common goals in place, they treat each other as part of the whole team machinery.

Looking at the team as a machine helps them understand that everybody has to have a job description. Some pieces are a bigger part of the machine than others. You may have one player who is an All-American and as the coach you build your offense or defense around him. But that only works if the rest of the players work together as a cohesive system.

A player needs to accept his role with the attitude of doing the best he can and adapting to that role as much as he possibly can. Throughout the season he should be asking himself how he is going to improve his part. What's the plan? You can't just walk through the woods and strike gold. You have to have an idea of what you want and how you are going to get there.

Any idiot can get people organized into a team, but getting interaction with good solid questions that make them think about what's important is daunting. Building a unified and consistently performing team requires constant attention to the individual players, the overall team, and the big picture for not only this year but also the years to come. We focus on our strengths and get better at those. We don't put much pie in the sky. We start with a realistic view of what we do well and what we need to improve upon and build from there.

The value systems of different players can create arguments. There might be a lineman who thinks he can hold onto the other guy's jersey even though the rule says he has to keep his palm out. He thinks he can look better or help us win if he can cheat.

That's part of what we try to teach them as we build the team: that it's about *all* of us, not just one individual. Some of these kids come from an environment of survival where it's get whatever you can for as little as possible, and if you can't, you take it. They aren't used to thinking of others first and themselves second. It's in these group discussions that the real foundation of the team is built one goal at a time.

As the groups work together to decide what best reflects their goals and values the coaches are roaming around the room helping them focus, raise questions, and remove anything that might be inappropriate or irrelevant. For the most part it's a hands-off process. We want the players to step up, be assertive, and learn to give their opinion, and then defend it to justify their feelings. I want the kids to learn to explain why they believe the way they do, and if they don't know why they believe, to start thinking about the deeper motivations.

At the end we never really come out with a definitive 'this is it.' We can have groups that create the same symbols, but with slightly different twists on the meanings and what the symbol represents.

When the groups are finished with the process the symbols are collected and I find an artist to put them together into a single coat of arms. When it's completed the drawing is put up in the locker room as a constant reminder. To me the coat of arms is kind of like your family crest. In the heat of the battle, in the anger, frustration, or jubilation of the moment, it's a visual reminder of what's really important and who you are as a team.

Every team, every season, has its own personality. We might add or subtract a couple of individuals who were very influential and because of that the group dynamic takes on a whole different personality. The results are never the same.

But the overall goal is—to mold these young people into something positive and productive adults. At the same time they are learning I want them to have fun and to enjoy the game. Football can be hard, hot, nasty work. It's not a game for the meek. I've seen a lot of these kids grow up, right there on the field. They figure out pretty quickly that they have to be tough no matter what position they play. Every single one of these guys has to be ready to strap it up and go to war.

But they'll do that knowing that the entire team has their back. This isn't just a group of kids who can run, kick, pass, and catch. It's a family.

Chapter 17

Everybody Has Their Role

Being head coach is a lot like being a CEO of a corporation. You're overseeing a couple hundred people with different talents and temperaments. You work with the coaching staff the same way you work with the players—look at their strengths and weaknesses, having a respect for their abilities, and a short-term memory for their shortcomings. Use directness and honesty with them at all times.

In 1973 I believed you should treat everybody the same but that's the exact opposite of the right approach. Adapt your management style to match the personality of the other person.

I like to run an organized ship. I have a list of thirty-plus things that need to be done. The list includes everything from getting helmets cleaned and putting stripes on the field to who's breaking down game film, who's doing the scouting report, who's writing the practice plan, and even who is washing jocks and socks.

I coach the coaches too in order to help them teach, manage, guide, direct, and communicate with the players. The wheel runs pretty smoothly as long as somebody doesn't try to do somebody else's job, or let his or her ego get in the way, or be critical in a derogatory way. When that happens things get out of whack and the whole team suffers.

I'm not one to call a meeting unless I have something to say. We don't have daily staff meetings. Some coaches meet daily whether or not they have anything to talk about. If I have something to say I'll call a meeting and put it on the table. I don't want to run a dictatorship. I want to hear their opinions and get their input.

Some people cut off communication to eliminate conflict, which creates bigger issues. You have to communicate. You have to hear opinions. And then with that information somebody has to make a final decision.

Ultimately it all comes back to rest on the head coach's shoulders. For example the defensive coordinator has to make the decisions about what the defense is doing, when they do it, and who is doing what on the field—but they do so with the head coach's blessing and approval.

Just as I do with the players, I make sure to find the right coaching talents for every job so the offense, defense, and special teams fit together seamlessly.

I have the coaching staff do a self-evaluation before I do my evaluation. We'll sit there and talk for a couple hours going through the whole gamut, pros, cons, things we needed to improve upon, and strengths we need to emphasize. If one of the staff has a negative attitude we're going to talk about how that is impacting the team and how they can improve their approach. If someone is avoiding conflict I want to know why and how we can get them to be more proactive.

I do this twice a year—in January and before starting spring practice so we can keep looking at how we can improve the program.

In return I evaluate myself and I share my strengths and weaknesses with them, and I want them to do the same for me. Some of them are more honest, some are fearful of being too honest. But I think if you can have open communication to share strengths and weaknesses, suggestions, communications, and building relationships, you have a chance to improve. Your lifeline as a head coach is whether you can do that and keep it fresh.

One of the most important questions I ask my staff is: "What have you done today to make us better? Is it communication with a player? Is it studying this or that?" I expect them to take initiative and to know their jobs. If someone comes to me with a problem they better have a possible solution too. I want them to think the problem through. The coaching staff gets paid to deal with conflict and handle issues, to overcome adversity as coaches, and to teach players to do the same. It's not going to be a bowl of cherries every day. Leading a team is a bumpy road and you have to find a way to smooth it out, make it productive, and still get to where you want to go.

My job doesn't end when the season ends. I'm not only responsible for things on the field, but also for everything that happens off the field, from recruitment to networking. I'm also working with the individual players, establishing relationships, trust, and communication with them. A lot of people think in the off-season, I'm out playing golf or fishing. I'm not. I'm still working for the team—only in the off-season it might be a 60-hour workweek instead of 100 plus.

At Saint Francis we haven't had much turnover in our coaching staff. In some programs it's a revolving door, half of them in and half of them out on an annual basis. Maybe it's because I think it's important to build good working relationships with my staff. I ask them to go out to lunch or to go get a beer after work. We've gone out for wings after staff meetings. It's good to get away from work once in a while and laugh together. When we're out like that we don't talk seriously about much. We just build our team. In a more informal way it serves the same purpose for coaches as our coat of arms exercise does for players. I've found over the years this helps everyone relax and creates a positive working environment.

There's a trickle-down effect from the coaches. If they are positive, strong leaders, we get a positive, strong team. I don't want to ever fire anyone as long as they've been loyal. I can deal with mistakes. I can deal with stupidity. But I can't deal with disloyalty. I've been lucky in the people I have hired. In the last thirty years I can count on one hand the number of people I've fired. I give them loyalty, they give it to me in return, and everyone benefits.

At this level of play there isn't much difference in ability from the top to the bottom, but there is a great disparity in terms of how it all works and fits together. You can match up equal teams in ability, but if one team doesn't have that true team mentality they won't be as successful. It matters more when you're playing for every one of the people around you, not just yourself.

President Harry Truman once said, "It's amazing how much can be accomplished when it doesn't matter who gets the credit." I think that's true for coaching; I think it's true for teams. When you're all working together you can deliver a mighty blow because everybody's doing whatever he can for the benefit of team in order to accomplish great things.

President Truman was probably talking in terms of World War II or the Korean War and his military leaders, but what he said is so true in everything else as well. When it's all about one person nothing reaches full potential.

That's not to say that we don't have a lot of outstanding athletes. We do. But they got there partly on talent and partly because of the collective team behind them.

Saint Francis won 102 victories in the first 10 years of its football program, and that was after posting a 2-8 record in our first season. In our first year we had all freshman, no direction, and we weren't quite sure where we were going.

We started with the mindset and understanding that everybody had a role, and we all had goals for the team. It was the first year we did the coat of arms. The success has been phenomenal. I'm very, very proud of the hard work every one of those players put in to make this team what it is today.

Chapter 18

Three Guiding Principles

Every moment is a teaching moment. Donley gives
instructions to the offense on the sidelines.

My life is governed by three simple principles: do what is right,

do what is best, and do to others what you would want others to do to you (also known as The Golden Rule). To me, the recipe for success is fairly simple—but it's one thing to know what's best and it's another thing to actually do it.

Do What is Right

This is all about making wise choices. If it isn't going to make you a better player, student, person then why do you choose to do it? Only do things that are going to improve your person, student self, and player self.

Don't cut classes or corners. Be on time, not late. Tell don't lie.

One of the biggest battles I face with players today is drugs. Society and culture promote drug use even though it's against the law. Our society is giving kids a clear message that it's okay to break the law. Our job as coaches and teachers is to teach these young men how to lead productive lives. Being responsible for their actions is a big part of that. It all starts with doing the right thing. That relates to everything in your life, from A to Z.

Do What Is Best

This is the commitment to excellence. Why do anything if you're not going to give it a hundred percent? Why punch the clock? Why walk out on the practice field, or watch the scoreboard clock to see when it's going to be over? Better not to do it at all than to approach it without every ounce of your energy.

It's all about snap to whistle, that interval between when the ball is put in play and the whistle signals the end of the play. That's when you clear your head and get it in the game.

On that field you have to block out girlfriends and everything else and focus on what is before you. When you are on the practice field you are focusing on the reason you are there—to get better. It's the same with the weight room and the classroom. Why go there and sit in the back row and fall asleep just to get credit for attendance.

If you always do what is best you might learn something that will make you a better person. If you are on a mission to become the best you can possibly be, in football and in life, it takes 100% commitment to do the very best you can do in all you do. Excellence isn't about the potential you are given but how you develop it physically and mentally. Excellence is about learning and understanding what commitment means. It's about always doing what is best.

It's not going to be easy. It's not always going to be fun. We're in a society that promotes doing whatever feels good and to avoid anything tough. That's not how it works in real life and not how it works on my football team.

Reporters would come up to me after we lost a big game and ask if I thought I set the goals too high or if my goals had been unrealistic. "Your goal every year is to win a national title, and you've never done it," the reporter used to say. "Maybe you're putting your players in an unrealistic situation."

I tell them the same thing every time. I never sell my players short. Our goal is always to be number one. It doesn't mean we will achieve that every time, but I believe if we set that goal, then we can direct all our efforts in that direction.

Champions don't gripe they look forward to the opportunity to go the extra mile so they can gain an edge. At Saint Francis our players have a motto: 'Above and beyond.' When they break out of a huddle they shout, "above and beyond." In order to achieve greatness you have to do more than go in and punch the clock, be there at work, go through the motions, and go home. You have to go above and beyond the call of duty. Doing your best means starting with an attitude that you can be the best.

The Golden Rule

Treat others the way you want to be treated with respect and dignity. A simple concept but sometimes hard to execute, especially when the road gets hard.

I believe this starts with developing relationships with players, customers, and fellow employees. To do that, you have to have good communication, which is 50% talking, but also 50% listening. So few of us are good listeners.

Along with that is trust and integrity. I once heard a wise man say, "If you have integrity that's all that matters, and if you don't have integrity, it's all that matters." That trust and integrity ripples outward from the players to the school, to the fans, to the supporters.

It's always a challenge to get young kids to see the importance of these principles. They're young, headstrong, and often foolish. They think they are invincible and this leads to a lot of stupid decisions. They think they can drink and drive; they won't crash. They can smoke dope; that's not going to affect them. They can cut classes and find a way to get through and pass. They believe they can put their lives on the edge and still be okay.

Maybe it's human nature, maybe it's a male quality, but many of us feel like we can walk on water. We can do those things and we don't have to do what everybody says. The real task is getting the people you are dealing with, coach and player, to grasp that fallacy.

It's the coaches' job to help young players see how important it is to work and accept their responsibility to the team. They have to feel like they will let down the group if they make bad choices.

We all do stupid things. I did when I was in college. But it's the coach's job to somehow get through the noise of that and channel all of their energy in the right direction. If you can teach them commitment and have loyalty to their teammates and to their coaches, it creates a bond. If you can then funnel that into a group guided by those three simple guiding principles then you've got something going."

At my first head-coaching job, I inherited the problem of a party going on every night and nobody caring. I could have taken the entire team to task. Instead I focused on one kid who was the biggest hell raiser of the group. I told him the program would continue in a downward spiral until one key individual—a player, not a coach—took the initiative and had the courage to step up to the group and say, "Here's where we are and this is the way it's going to be."

He was a tough kid, hard and unbreakable, who later ended up an All-American. A few days after I talked to him this kid stood up at a team meeting. He told the rest of the team that he was guiltier than anybody with focusing on parties and women instead of football. He told them, "Here's the deal. You're not going to see me doing this. I'm going to do what Coach says because I believe he's on to something."

He told them if they wanted to win they had to do the things the coach wanted. Then he added, "You've got my commitment, and if any of you cross the line I will personally beat it out of you." That commitment of one key player helped turn the corner for the whole team and I ended up having a winning season with that team.

Saint Francis has a rule for their coaching staff that says you complement publicly and you criticize privately. I believe in this. I have never seen the win in calling one kid out in front of the entire team.

When a player comes into my office everything else stops. My players never interrupt my work because they are my work.

Coaches sometimes think, "I don't like this kid, he's a pain in the ass, I have to get rid of him." Maybe that's so—or maybe there's something else at the core of that kid's behavior, like pressures from home or school. Give these kids the benefit of the doubt, give them guidelines and expectations, and try to help them succeed. Some you can't turn around, and some-times you have to make the hard decision to let them go.

It's just as important to have good leadership, as it is to have good players. I see leadership in all different sizes, shapes, and personality types. The best leaders aren't always Type-A, driven people. I've had some great leaders who were Type-B kids, not aggressive, a little introverted. They led by example. They didn't say much but when they did others listened.

For our coaches, Saint Francis has several coaching commandments:

1. Don't bitch about the players; they're the only ones we have

2. Develop short-term memory concerning players past mistakes, hold no grudges, and move on

3. Don't ever bad-mouth another coach publicly or to other staff members. If there is an issue, confront that coach or discuss with head football coach

4. Be a problem solver not a problem discoverer, and certainly not a problem creator

5. Find a way to overcome all adversity and make it the opportunity of a lifetime.

The real mark of leadership is the courage to deal with off-the-field issues without hiding or running from them. I had one kid, Jeff Wedding, who was the 2007 team leader. He was a humble, quiet individual, but when it came time to step up, Jeff did. I still get emails from parents who say Jeff inspired their sons in a positive way. That to me is what a good leader does.

It's not easy to get nineteen and twenty-year-old kids to make wise choices. I just keep bringing them back to those three guiding principles—the more you follow those, the more success you will have. If they see it in action, they believe it, and they follow suit.

I don't hammer on these kids all the time. I joke with them, I get to know them on a personal level. I want them to have fun, but also know that when I say something I mean it. I try to be positive because life's too short to be anything else.

The journey to success is a long, winding, hilly road that begins in the weight room in January. It continues with academic success in the classroom. It keeps going with spring practice, attitude development, and what happens between May and August when camp starts. If you do all that right when you get to the field in the fall you've got a team that truly works together.

Chapter 19

Making a Difference

I sat on that plane in 2004 certain I was going to die. I prayed to survive, to have a chance to change my life, to become the man God wanted me to be. I hope I have done that, and if I have, I have the University of Saint Francis and all the football players that have come through our program to thank for it.

In the years before I came to USF I had faced a whole lot of adversity. I'd been knocked down, time and again. I could have quit, could have gone into… I don't know, shoe sales instead, but I didn't. I got up and kept going.

In 2007, after the team lost their first regular season game since 2001 at Ohio Dominican, I pulled them together in the locker room after the game posed a question to them. "What are you going to do now? Are you going to cry in your beer and sulk or point a finger, saying who's at fault, or do you evaluate yourself? What could I have done better? How did I let myself down? How did I let the rest of this team down? And if any of you can answer 'I've done everything in my power' then you are on the right track, and if not, what are you going to do to change it? There are no cutting corners to achieving great things. There is no easy way."

The young men who have come through this program have learned that. They have given me their all on the field, and it shows in the wins we have stacked up. I don't ask them for perfection; I ask them for perseverance and heart.

No one is perfect, and frankly, I don't want to be around anyone who is. I'm sure as hell not perfect myself.

When I was sitting in that first ramshackle office with the lights flickering and the future uncertain, I asked myself why I was there. What's the real purpose? What the heck am I doing?

And then the light came on—literally and figuratively. I was there to make a difference. Not just to those kids, but to myself. It has been a process to figure out what that difference is and I certainly haven't gotten it all figured out yet, but with each year that passes I get a better handle on what's important.

I'm evaluated by my wins and losses. Whether I made it to the championship level or not. The big picture, however, is about so much more. Are we achieving our mission? Are we reaching our goals? Are we bringing pride to our school, our community, and are we people that we can be proud of at the end of the day?

When you're winning in the upper 97-98% of college football one or two losses is considered a bad year. We've created a monster in that respect. It's a good problem to have, but also allows a cruise control because 'you know' you're going to be good. The public knows you're going to be good. So you kind of get bored. You need challenges.

I'll go out and work hard to find some games against teams of a higher caliber. I love that challenge, and would love to take it further. Like playing Indiana University or Notre Dame—those would be dream games.

In the end it's the kids I remember. It's the kids I do this for. The best part for me is when an alum stays in touch and tells me they've really succeeded in life. I was in a local restaurant having dinner with a friend one night and Centennial Wireless (now part of ATT) was having an awards dinner in the banquet room. In walked three executives from Centennial, two of them were former players. Trent Scott graduated in the spring of 2002 and was then one of the top five or six executives in the company. Nick Bontempo was a 4.0 student and had graduated the previous year. Both these kids came over, embraced us and talked. Later when Scott did a workshop with the University of Saint Francis business department he told them he wouldn't be where he was today without that experience and the leadership skills he learned from being involved with the football program. That's what I do this for—for those young men.

It's not all me, not by any stretch. It's the school, it's the fans, and it's the entire football department. The football program at the University of Saint Francis is special, not just to us, but to every person in the stands. To appreciate that you only need to attend a home game and experience the aura of the place for yourself.

This university has completed me as a person. When I was young, I was a dreamer. I had no idea that my dream of coaching at a little Catholic school in Northern Indiana would turn into a career in Fort Wayne, a career that has enriched my life in a thousand ways.

When I didn't have a job and I had to start all over it was a humbling experience. I went from being on top to an all-time low. That time made me stronger and it really helped me put things in perspective. You can get all the glamour and glitter and accolades, but what's important is what you are making of this one life you have been given.

People ask me what I'm going to do when I retire. I'm a realist. I look down the road and think about how long I'm going to be able to physically do this. As for what's next? To me, it boils down to the same thing I ask my players: What can I do at that point in my life to be the best person I can be? To be the person God wants me to be? To be the man I asked Him to help me become?

I will always feel a special bond with the University of Saint Francis, and with its football program. I bleed blue. I've had opportunities to go elsewhere, Saint Francis is an integral part of my life. No, it's more than that. It's part of my family.

***

Coach Donley with QB Nick Ferrer after leading
Saint Francis's to their second consecutive national
championship over Reinhardt in December 2017.
Photo courtesy Reggie Hayes of the News-Sentinel

How would I like to be remembered? I would like to be
known for being a good man that cared about other people
that dedicated his life to helping young people become the
best they could be. I'd like to win another national title or
two but can't do that without that goal. I've worked awfully
hard trying to push the right buttons for people to become the
best they could be. I've never really expected much in return.
It's rewarding to me if I can see someone achieve and do well,

to be a great contributor to society as well as contributing to a football team. I hope in my eulogy people will think I was a pretty good coach, but the most important would be that. Some of the most important learning experiences we have in life are ones that aren't so pleasant.

Helping kids find ways to overcome the most adverse circumstances in life, every adversity. The one that probably affected my life more than any was when I didn't have a job and having to start over. I went from being on top to an all time low. It made me stronger. I learned a lot from it. I was really able to put things in perspective. You can get all the glamour and glitter and start believing all the stuff around you, but the bottom line is what you are doing right now. How you are dealing with circumstances, and what are making of your everyday life.

About the Author

Kevin Donley has experienced life's highs and lows. He was a young and successful coach with a national championship to his credit when his world collapsed and he found himself homeless, unemployed and no prospects for the future. This book takes you on his journey of learning from mistakes, rediscovering purpose, and never, never, ever, giving up on his dream.